NEW DIRECTIONS FOR STUDENT SERVICES

John H. Schuh, *Iowa State University*
EDITOR-IN-CHIEF

Elizabeth J. Whitt, *University of Iowa*
ASSOCIATE EDITOR

Student Affairs Research, Evaluation, and Assessment: Structure and Practice in an Era of Change

Gary D. Malaney
Student Affairs Research, Information, and Systems

EDITOR

Number 85, Spring 1999

JOSSEY-BASS PUBLISHERS
San Francisco

STUDENT AFFAIRS RESEARCH, EVALUATION, AND ASSESSMENT: STRUCTURE
AND PRACTICE IN AN ERA OF CHANGE
Gary D. Malaney (ed.)
New Directions for Student Services, no. 85
John H. Schuh, Editor-in-Chief
Elizabeth J. Whitt, Associate Editor

Microfilm copies of issues and articles are available in 16mm and 35mm,
as well as microfiche in 105mm, through University Microfilms Inc., 300
North Zeeb Road, Ann Arbor, Michigan 48106–1346.

ISSN 0164-7970   ISBN 0-7879-4216-2

NEW DIRECTIONS FOR STUDENT SERVICES is part of The Jossey-Bass Higher
and Adult Education Series and is published quarterly by Jossey-Bass Inc.,
Publishers, 350 Sansome Street, San Francisco, California 94104–1342.
Periodicals postage paid at San Francisco, California, and at additional
mailing offices. Postmaster: Send address changes to New Directions for
Student Services, Jossey-Bass Inc., Publishers, 350 Sansome Street, San
Francisco, California 94104–1342.

New Directions for Student Services is indexed in College Student Personnel Abstracts and Contents Pages in Education.

SUBSCRIPTIONS cost $56.00 for individuals and $99.00 for institutions,
agencies, and libraries. See ordering information page at end of book.

EDITORIAL CORRESPONDENCE should be sent to the Editor-in-Chief,
John H. Schuh, N 243 Lagomarcino Hall, Iowa State University, Ames,
Iowa, 50011

Cover photograph by Wernher Krutein/PHOTOVAULT © 1990.

Jossey-Bass Web address: www.josseybass.com

Printed in the United States of America on acid-free recycled paper containing 100 percent recovered waste paper, of which at least 20 percent is
postconsumer waste.

Contents

Editor's Notes

In institutions of higher education, research activities may be conducted by various individuals in different departments within student affairs. Although much of that activity is discussed within this volume, the primary focus is on the student affairs research office, a centralized function within the entire division of student affairs. The "office" may consist of only one person, but the primary responsibility of that person is research for student affairs. While an office may indeed be located centrally within the division of student affairs, it also is likely to be within a department of student affairs, such as admissions.

As I note in the first chapter, one of the most difficult tasks in studying student affairs research offices is actually locating such offices. On the surface, one might think this should be an easy task, especially when national organizations such as the American College Personnel Association (ACPA) and the National Association of Student Personnel Administrators (NASPA) have major research divisions within their organizations. However, given the number of institutions of higher education, it is easy to see how maintaining accurate records is nearly impossible. After all, not all institutions are members of these national organizations. And the people in the institutions who participate in the organizations are not necessarily the researchers. One might note that there also has never been a completely accurate count of higher education or student affairs graduate programs in this country either.

At any rate, this volume represents the first attempt actually to describe what student affairs researchers across the country do on the job. In Chapter One, I provide an overview of what is happening across the country based on the results of my 1995 national study of thirty-five student affairs research offices. In that chapter, I discuss where the offices are located, who runs the offices, how the offices are organized, and what types of research functions are performed.

The next two chapters provide inside views of the workings of two offices. The authors of these chapters not only detail the types of research they have conducted, but they discuss how institutional reorganizations have affected their student affairs research missions. In Chapter Two, Linda Moxley looks at how the University of Texas at Arlington has addressed its needs for information pertaining to student affairs and the relationship to a newly created institutional research office. In Chapter Three, Anthony Bajdek and Sungwoo Kim give a detailed account of the types of research they conducted before and after the student affairs research enterprise was shut down at Northeastern University because of institutional downsizing.

In Chapter Four, Gwendolyn Dungy provides an important discussion of student affairs research in the community college environment. Although community colleges generally do not have student affairs research offices, they still have a great need for student-related research. Through a series of personal conversations with several community college leaders, the author offers some interesting insights regarding student-related research at community colleges.

In Chapter Five, Gary Hanson introduces what he calls a new role for student affairs research. He defines policy analysis research as the design, collection, analysis, and dissemination of data and/or information for the purpose of creating or modifying educational policy. He gives a careful description of such research in relation to a specific scholarship award policy at the University of Texas at Austin.

Chapter Six provides advice regarding the application of specific technologies to aid student affairs researchers. Elizabeth Williams and Cary Anderson discuss a variety of computer applications such as the World Wide Web and Listservs that can be used to find data and information. They also discuss individual software and hardware that can aid researchers in their day-to-day work in survey design and administration.

In Chapter Seven, Kevin Grennan and Margaret Jablonski discuss how divisions of student affairs, especially those without research expertise on staff, might collaborate with faculty members in their institutions to develop a research agenda. These authors also discuss how higher education graduate programs might better assist divisions of student affairs in their research missions.

In Chapter Eight, Thomas Hadley looks beyond the simple acts of data collection and report writing of student affairs research offices as he encourages student affairs researchers to use their positions to become what he calls information brokers. He suggests that as information brokers, we need to help student affairs and the institution as a whole become *learning organizations*, as described by Peter Senge (1990). In particular, we need to learn to expand our focus from narrow departmental research and small pieces of the student experience to broader institutional concerns and the totality of the student learning experience.

Finally, in Chapter Nine, I suggest a few resources that should help guide both experienced student affairs researchers and individuals that are just getting started. These resources include books and sites on the World Wide Web.

Gary D. Malaney

Editor

Reference

Senge, P. M. *The Fifth Discipline: The Art and Practice of the Learning Organization.* New York: Doubleday, 1990.

GARY D. MALANEY is director of Student Affairs Research, Information, and Systems (SARIS) and associate professor of higher education at the University of Massachusetts Amherst.

The activities of student affairs research offices are discussed.

The Structure and Function of Student Affairs Research Offices: A National Study

Gary D. Malaney

For some researchers, student affairs research is considered to be a proliferation of institutional research (IR) (Hearn and Corcoran, 1988). These authors argue that IR is increasingly being decentralized into other units on campus for one or both of the following reasons: (1) the claims of the centralized IR office are not accepted as legitimate across campus, or (2) the time and resources of the IR office are insufficient to meet the needs of the entire campus constituency. For student affairs research, it appears that the latter is clearly the case. Although much student-related research is conducted in IR offices, these offices have very broad missions, much of which has little to do with student affairs issues. It is more likely that the academic concerns of the provost's or president's office will take precedence over the concerns of student affairs administrators. If the housing director wants to evaluate a diversity training program in the residence halls, how likely is it that the IR office will be able to assist? If the student activities director wants to conduct a survey of students to ascertain their needs and interest for programs and activities, will the IR office be able to administer the survey? More likely than not, the answers to these questions will be "No."

In recent years, several scholars and researchers have discussed the importance of conducting research in student affairs (Beeler and Hunter, 1991; Beeler and Oblander, 1989; Brown, 1986; Johnson and Steele, 1984; Kuh, 1979; Malaney and Weitzer, 1993; Thurman and Malaney, 1989), but there has been little emphasis on the work of individual student affairs research offices (Malaney, 1993; Moxley, 1988). Although one might argue that assessment and evaluation, not "research," are the real foci of such offices, even the latest assessment manifesto (Upcraft and Schuh, 1996), though an excellent resource, fails to discuss in any detail the work of student affairs research offices.

The lack of emphasis on student affairs research offices in prior literature is probably due in part to the fact that the number of such offices is small. Johnson and Steele (1984) and Beeler and Oblander (1989) found that only 12 percent of the colleges and universities reported having a student affairs office whose main function was research. And a follow-up by Karl Beeler on those 12 percent of the respondents in his study produced a list of only 26 institutions (4.6 percent of the sample) having a true student affairs research office, meaning an office consisting of at least one person whose primary responsibility was conducting student affairs research.

Given resources and research expertise, there is a large variety of evaluation and assessment activities that student affairs divisions would conduct. Almost twenty years ago, Kuh (1979) argued that such activity should be conducted in student affairs research and evaluation offices, and today, existing offices are conducting such studies (Malaney, 1993; Moxley, 1988). Until the study described in this chapter was undertaken, Malaney and Moxley provided the only documented accounts of individual offices. The purpose of this study is to provide a more detailed account of all known centralized student affairs research operations. *Centralized* is a key term, because like the proliferation of IR activities into other campus offices such as student affairs, student affairs itself has seen a proliferation of its own research activities into other student affairs offices, such as admissions, housing, and career services. The focus of this study was on the centralized research activity within student affairs, even though that activity may be housed in a decentralized student affairs office and not be under the direct purview of the senior student affairs officer (SSAO).

Method

One might think that locating student affairs research offices would be an easy task, especially when the two major national organizations, American College Personnel Association (ACPA) and National Association of Student Personnel Administrators (NASPA), have research divisions as part of their structures. But before this study, no one had ever compiled a list of such offices. In the spring of 1994, inquiries were sent to the individuals on the Beeler-Oblander list to update their information and provide names of other possible student affairs research offices; as a result, a few changes and additions were made. Announcements also were posted on two student affairs listservs, CSPTALK and NASPA-I, which garnered a few more additions to the list. Discussions at ACPA and NASPA conferences were helpful in expanding the list, as was an announcement in *Passages,* the newsletter of ACPA's Commission IX on Assessment for Student Development. By winter 1995, all of these inquiries yielded a list of only thirty-nine offices.

In April 1995, a survey instrument was mailed to all of the offices on the list. After three follow-ups during the summer of 1995, responses were obtained from thirty-seven offices. Of those thirty-seven responses, two had to be excluded: One had recently been transferred to academic affairs and the other had been eliminated due to campus budget reductions. This meant that thirty-five out of thirty-seven possible offices returned usable surveys, for a response rate of 95 percent.

Results

The results of the study are discussed in three separate sections. First, the backgrounds of the respondents to the survey are described both in terms of the offices and the individuals in charge of the offices. Next, the organized structure and budgets of the offices are discussed. And finally, the functions of the offices are presented.

The Respondents—Where They Are and Who They Are. In the study by Beeler and Oblander (1989), all except one of the twenty-six student affairs research offices were located in research or doctoral institutions as defined by the Carnegie classification scheme. Although those offices are included in this study and clearly make up the majority of offices, a substantial number of offices are located in other types of institutions. The breakdown of the thirty-seven offices by institutional type is as follows: fifteen research-I, six research-II, three doctoral-I, two doctoral-II, ten masters-I, and one baccalaureate-I. All except three of these institutions are public institutions.

As Figure 1.1 shows, the offices also are fairly well spread out across the country. Eight are located in the West, with five in California and one each in Arizona, Hawaii, and Washington. Five are in the Midwest, with one each in North Dakota, Nebraska, Colorado, Oklahoma, and Missouri. Seven are in the Mideast, with three in Ohio, two in Illinois, and one each in Michigan and Minnesota. Twelve are in the South, with five in North Carolina, three in Texas, and one each in Arkansas, Alabama, South Carolina, and Virginia. And finally, five are in the Northeast, with two in Maryland and one each in Pennsylvania, New York, and Massachusetts.

The individuals in charge of the research operations have varying job titles, but the most common title is director ($n = 15$), followed by assistant or associate vice chancellor or vice president ($n = 6$) and coordinator ($n = 4$). Other titles include dean, assistant to the vice chancellor or vice president, and research assistant or associate. As one might expect, all of the respondents have advanced degrees. Of the thirty-one respondents who completed the education section of the survey, twenty-five have doctorates and six have master's degrees as their highest degree. The respondents' doctoral degrees are in the following fields: higher education ($n = 10$), psychology/applied psychology ($n = 8$), educational psychology or counseling psychology ($n = 3$), educational administration ($n = 1$), sociology ($n = 1$), political science ($n = 1$), and English

Figure 1.1. Location of Student Affairs Research Offices

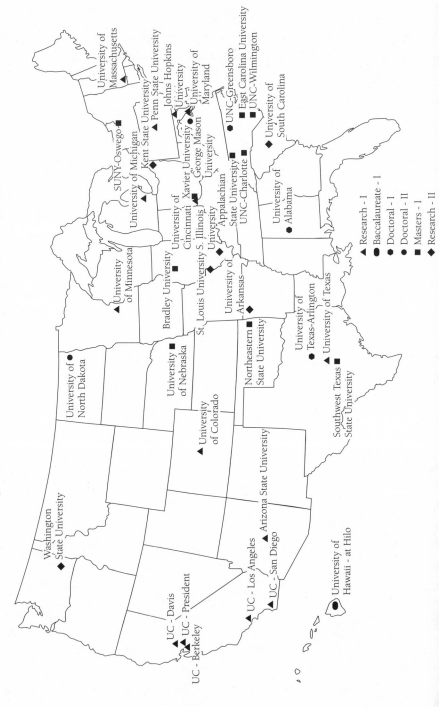

($n = 1$). The median actual reported salary (or midpoint of the reported range) of the person in charge of a research office was $50,125 ($n = 28$).

How They Are Organized. Respondents were asked to indicate, by title, to whom they reported. Thirty-one of the positions were highly centralized within the student affairs organization, with twenty reporting directly to the SSAO (of which fifteen were titled vice chancellor/president), six reporting to an associate vice chancellor, and five reporting to an assistant vice chancellor.

Though a few of the offices are quite large, the typical office is a one-person shop working on a shoestring budget. Twenty-one respondents reported that their offices consist of one professional (not necessarily full-time) with little or no support staff. (A few of these offices had some part-time clerical or student help.) Five other offices consist of only one professional but also have at least one full-time equivalent (FTE) of clerical or student support. The median annual budget for the thirty-one offices that reported budgetary data was $65,000, which included staff salaries.

Thirty of the respondents answered an open-ended question about how the research operation's budget has fluctuated and had an impact on research activities in the past five years. Three of the offices were relatively new and thus had stable budgets. Several of the small offices actually have no operating budgets, and they receive money to do projects on an "as needed" basis. Consequently, most of this group reported level-funded budgets. In total, thirteen of the thirty respondents reported that their budgets had remained stable over the past five years. Two other offices actually reported increases; however, fifteen offices reported budget cuts. Reductions were clearly the norm for the largest offices, some of which reported budget cuts of between 20 to 40 percent, resulting in staff reductions, fewer computer upgrades, more contract and grant work, and less research conducted overall. Of course, many of these cuts can be attributed to budget reductions suffered by most public higher education systems across the country during the few years preceding this study.

Respondents were asked several questions about research administration. Generally the person in charge of the student affairs research office determines what type of research is conducted ($n = 21$). Others reported that the SSAO ($n = 7$), committee ($n = 1$), or someone else ($n = 6$) has that primary responsibility. Respondents reported working with various other campus constituencies when conducting research. Of course, all offices reported working with other student affairs offices, but thirty-three respondents reported working with other administrative offices outside of student affairs and twenty-six reported working with academic departments. Interestingly, only nineteen offices reported working with student organizations.

What They Do. Not surprisingly, survey research is the dominant research method for most offices; mail surveys are more popular than telephone surveys. All thirty-five offices have conducted survey research within the past two years; thirty-four have conducted mail surveys and twenty-four have conducted telephone surveys. A variety of other research methods also were used in the past two years: institutional database analysis ($n = 32$), focus groups (n = 21), content analysis (n = 16), observational studies (n = 9), and experiments (n = 7).

All of the offices conduct surveys of both on- and off-campus students, and twenty-three offices conduct surveys of graduate students. Eighteen offices also conduct surveys of faculty and staff. Twelve offices conduct surveys of other colleges and universities, and three offices conduct surveys of local community residents. The number of surveys conducted by each office varies considerably: from zero to twenty telephone surveys per academic year (median = 1.5) and from zero to thirty mail surveys per academic year (median = two).

Respondents were asked a few other questions about the type of research activities they undertake. For instance, they were asked about conducting Total Quality Management (TQM)-related research on campus. It turns out that nineteen of the campuses are engaged in TQM initiatives, but only six of the offices have conducted research related to those initiatives. Program evaluation studies are fairly popular; twenty-seven of the offices conducted such studies within the past two years. Interestingly, a few of the offices have conducted some larger scale studies within the past two years: eight conducted statewide studies, three conducted regional or multistate studies, and five conducted national studies.

In terms of disseminating results, most offices (n = 23) prepare formal written reports and do oral presentations on campus. All offices routinely report findings to the SSAO and the office or person who requested the study. Thirty offices report findings to the general campus community. Eleven offices report their findings to the local media, and fifteen offices report findings to interested parties across the country.

Respondents also were asked about the scholarly use of their offices' data. Twenty respondents reported that their research findings have been presented at professional or scholarly meetings or conferences in the past two years. These meetings include the Association for the Study of Higher Education, American Association for Higher Education, Association for Institutional Research, NASPA, and ACPA. Nine respondents reported that their findings have been published in scholarly journals in the past two years. The journals include *NASPA Journal, Research in Higher Education, Journal of College Student Development, College Student Affairs Journal,* and *Journal of Freshman Year Experience.*

Conclusion

Positive and negative indicators stem from this study. From a student affairs view, the biggest negative is that such a small number of student affairs research offices could be found. Although there may be a few more offices out there, it is unlikely that the number is large. What does that say about the profession? Perhaps one of the respondents said it best: "I know there is within student affairs a misunderstanding or a dislike of research and program evaluation. . . . I wonder how strong these feelings are on other campuses. . . . I suppose the fact that there are so few 'researchers' in student affairs says something about the acceptance–lack of acceptance.

The "misunderstanding" or "dislike" of research is likely to be due in part to the lack of emphasis placed on research in student affairs graduate programs. Although Hunter and Beeler (1991) and Brown (1991) have recognized the need for graduate programs to do more within their curricula, they also realize that adding a course or two in research will not create researchers. Graduate programs have a wide agenda, and research is but one competency area to be addressed within a typical twelve- to sixteen-course structure for a master's program. Doctoral programs can be (and should be) somewhat more focused on research, but too often a two-course requirement is all that is expected in those programs as well. This background hardly prepares one to do a dissertation, let alone focus on research as a career. Accordingly, Hunter and Beeler, as well as Brown, have called for graduate programs to form partnerships with practitioners to build research expertise within student affairs. If a student affairs research office could be developed at each institution housing a student affairs graduate program, the number of offices across the country would triple. Graduate programs might then focus on helping other local colleges in their surrounding areas.

Another negative finding uncovered by this study is the extent of the budget cuts suffered by some of the offices. At least two major student affairs research operations were eliminated in the past five years. Fortunately, the office at Bowling Green State University, home of a major student affairs graduate preparation program, has been reinstated. Although the other office has experienced some revitalization thanks to a new president, it has not been fully restored. The former head of that office indicated that his office existed from 1984 to 1991, and in 1991 the university retrenchment eliminated 200 positions. He noted, "I guess that our research was deemed to be no longer necessary given financial exigencies."

This study does offer several reasons to be encouraged. For instance, fifteen of the offices in this study were created within the past five years, a time of serious budget retrenchment in institutions of higher education across the country. It also is encouraging that thirty-one of the offices in this study exist on campuses that additionally house offices of institutional research. One might assume that those campuses truly value the student affairs research perspective. This is not to say that campuses that run student-based research out of their IR offices do not appreciate such research. Usually, the perspectives and emphases are just different when the office is housed in academic affairs or the president's office versus student affairs.

Another positive finding is that current interest in student affairs research seems to be quite high. Over the past seven years, several individuals from campuses across the country have approached this author about starting student affairs research programs. Some of those new programs are represented in this study. Conversations at national student affairs conferences have indicated strong interest and support for student affairs research offices. The current

NASPA executive director Gwen Dungy is extremely high on student affairs research. All of these indicators point positively in the future direction of student affairs research.

References

Beeler, K. J., and Hunter, D. E. *Puzzles and Pieces in Wonderland: The Promise and Practice of Student Affairs Research.* Washington, D.C.: National Association of Student Personnel Administrators, 1991.

Beeler, K. J., and Oblander, F. W. *A Study of Student Affairs Research and Evaluation Activities in American Colleges and Universities.* Washington, D.C.: National Association of Student Personnel Administrators, 1989.

Brown, R. D. "Research: A Frill or an Obligation?" *Journal of College Student Personnel,* 1986, 27, 195.

Brown, R. D. "Student Affairs Research on Trial." In K. J. Beeler and D. E. Hunter (eds.), *Puzzles and Pieces in Wonderland: The Promise and Practice of Student Affairs Research.* Washington, D.C.: National Association of Student Personnel Administrators, 1991.

Hearn, J. C., and Corcoran, M. E. "An Exploration of Factors Behind the Proliferation of the Institutional Research Enterprise." *Journal of Higher Education,* 1988, 59, 634–651.

Hunter, D. E., and Beeler, K. J. "Peering Through the 'Looking Glass' at Preparation Needed for Student Affairs Research." In K. J. Beeler and D. E. Hunter (eds.), *Puzzles and Pieces in Wonderland: The Promise and Practice of Student Affairs Research.* Washington, D.C.: National Association of Student Personnel Administrators, 1991.

Johnson, D. H., and Steele, B. H. "A National Survey of Research Activity and Attitudes in Student Affairs Divisions." *Journal of College Student Personnel,* 1984, 25, 200–205.

Kuh, G. D. *Evaluation in Student Affairs.* Cincinnati, Ohio: ACPA Media, 1979.

Malaney, G. D. "A Comprehensive Student Affairs Research Office." *NASPA Journal,* 1993, 30, 182–189.

Malaney, G. D., and Weitzer, W. H. "Research on Students: A Framework of Methods Based on Cost and Expertise. *NASPA Journal,* 1993, 30, 126–137.

Moxley, L. S. "The Role and Impact of a Student Affairs Research and Evaluation Office." *NASPA Journal,* 1988, 25, 174–179.

Thurman, Q., and Malaney, G. D. "Surveying Students as a Means of Assessing and Changing Policies and Practices of Student Affairs Programs. *NASPA Journal,* 1989, 27, 101–107.

Upcraft, M. L., and Schuh, J. H. *Assessment in Student Affairs: A Guide for Practitioners.* San Francisco: Jossey-Bass, 1996.

GARY D. MALANEY *is director of Student Affairs Research, Information, and Systems (SARIS) and associate professor of higher education at the University of Massachusetts Amherst.*

Information concerning student body characteristics, program evaluations, and student development outcomes is essential for student affairs planning, budget development, program improvement, and reaccreditation purposes. This chapter examines how the University of Texas at Arlington's (UTA) Student Affairs Division has addressed its needs for information.

Student Affairs Research and Evaluation: An Inside View

Linda S. Moxley

In 1981, in the absence of an institutional research office, the University of Texas at Arlington's vice president for student affairs established a research and evaluation office. Demands for accountability, the need to make decisions on the basis of facts, the desire maximally to respond to students' needs and preferences, and a keen interest in wisely using the division's financial resources and personnel talents were forces and factors that prompted the creation of the unit. As time permitted, research and evaluation requests from other on-campus units were addressed (Moxley, 1988).

Over the years, the Student Affairs Research and Evaluation Office's reputation for quality research was recognized on campus and nationally. In 1986, the Southern Association of Colleges and Schools (SACS) Reaffirmation Committee commended the unit, recognized its role in program improvement, and stated that it "seems to be on the cutting edge of administration" (Ezell and others, 1986, p. 30). By 1990, the office staff had expanded to include a director, two professional researchers, an administrative secretary, two graduate research assistants, and two programmer analysts who provided computer-related support for the Student Affairs Division. Then, three years later, in 1993, the university's new president and new provost further strengthened the university's commitment to planning and the use of management information by requesting the director of the Student Affairs Research and Evaluation Office to form and direct an Office of Institutional Research and Planning (IR&P), which would report to the provost.

With the chief student affairs researcher at the helm, the Student Affairs Research and Evaluation Office was merged with the external reports section of the Registrar's Office to form the IR&P Office. In less than a year, considerable progress had been made. Research needs were identified university-wide; goals,

New Directions for Student Services, no. 85, Spring 1999 © Jossey-Bass Publishers

11

objectives, and time frames were established; additional data verification procedures were put into place; for the first time, internal and external reports were generated from a common database; and the university's first fact book was produced with all publication expenses assumed by an off-campus vendor. It was then, after the IR&P Office had an established direction, that the director made the decision to return to Student Affairs to champion the division's research and planning efforts in the absence of a formal support staff. Back in Student Affairs as the assistant vice president, the former researcher shouldered many roles in addition to coordinating planning and research (for example, staff development, marketing, publications, fund raising).

The recently hired president and provost served the university for less than two years when, in 1995, they received votes of no confidence from the faculty and ultimately were removed from their positions. This was a critical time for the university, since the SACS reaccreditation visit, which occurs every ten years, was scheduled for 1996. A new president and provost were hired and were able to postpone the visit for a year.

Then, in 1997, four years after Student Affairs had surrendered its research and evaluation unit, it received its second highly valued commendation from the Southern Association of Colleges and Schools Reaffirmation Committee. The Committee's report stated: "The Division has given a great deal of effort to the development of clearly stated goals and objectives within the mission and purpose of the Division. The [self-study] report and other documents give evidence that regular assessment procedures are in place in all areas. The Division is to be commended for the truly professional and comprehensive scope of its research and evaluation efforts (Commission on Colleges, 1997, p. 66).

These highly prized commendations suggest that student affairs divisions can effectively plan, research, and evaluate with diverse organizational structures like a student affairs research and evaluation office or a staff member providing consultation and coordination division-wide. However, planning and research efforts are only effective if research and evaluation technical expertise resides within the division and the chief student affairs administrator and campus president support the concepts of planning and evaluation and utilize the information generated.

Several principles underlie the successful planning, research, and information utilization in UTA's Student Affairs Division: (1) a systematic information-driven planning process that promotes improvement of programs and services, (2) a collaborative approach among the full-range of data collectors, (3) the creative pursuit of practical data collection approaches, and (4) the gathering of progressively sophisticated data.

Information Is Required for Effectiveness

Information is the pivotal component that propels UTA's student affairs planning process into a continuous loop that yields increased effectiveness. Figure 2.1 shows the basic planning process used to promote effectiveness within

Figure 2.1. A Student Affairs Planning Model

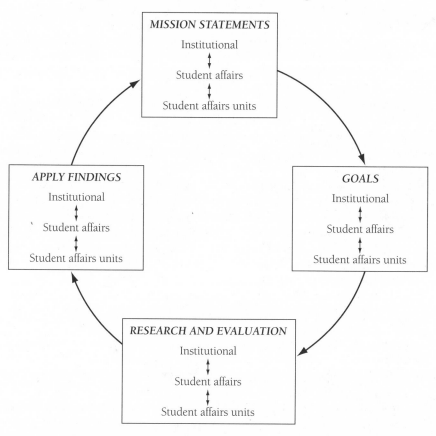

UTA's Student Affairs Division. Student affairs goals, objectives, and action strategies are clearly linked to the university and division's missions and are shaped by information about student needs, goals, and characteristics. Similarly, student affairs departmental goals and objectives are shaped by student- and program-related information; they help accomplish division goals, and are linked to the university and division's missions. At regular intervals, evaluation data are collected to determine the level of goal achievement. The findings are applied to define the next series of goals, objectives, and strategies. Periodically, the information gathered prompts a refocusing of mission statements at various levels; but most definitely, the database analyses, evaluation, and research findings are used to redefine goals, objectives, and strategies that in turn increase the effectiveness of the division's programs, services, policies, procedures, and personnel.

This fundamental scheme (that is, establishing goals and objectives to achieve the organization's and the division's missions, evaluating goal achievement, and applying the findings for improvement) has prevailed in various forms in the management literature. And it is a primary focus when the Southern Association of Colleges and Schools' peer review teams make campus visits for the purpose of accreditation/reaccreditation (Commission on Colleges, 1996).

Collaboration Among Data Collectors

Student affairs divisions have employed a wide range of informal and formal structures for collecting information, including (1) a professionally staffed student affairs research and evaluation office; (2) a central administrator (for example, vice president, dean, associate, or assistant vice president or dean) conducting or coordinating research as one of several responsibilities; (3) a representative committee; (4) departmental research coordinators; and (5) individual staff members who collect data for personal or professional reasons; for example, to fulfill academic course or funding agency requirements. The research skills and interest of staff members, financial resources, existence of a campus research office, and the extent to which the chief student affairs administrator and president see student- and program-related information as a priority, all have an impact on the data collection structure(s) selected.

To maximize the number of research and evaluation efforts undertaken, the student affairs research component at UTA (initially the formal research office and later the central administrator) takes advantage of all possible support systems. Assistance from all levels and departments of the division are employed. Some staff members assist with instrument development, some use their academic classes for survey administration, and others provide student employees to help with survey collation or telephone interviewing.

Valuable data collection resources also are available beyond the student affairs division. Faculty and students in pertinent undergraduate and graduate programs (for example, higher education administration, college student personnel, counseling, psychology, and sociology) are often interested in collecting student-based data, particularly when financial support is available. Graduate student research–based internships and master's and doctoral research can provide much needed information. However, caution must be exercised to ensure that the practitioner's needs are addressed and that the time spent supervising does not exceed the benefits.

Forming a relationship with information-rich administrative offices may be even more productive. Partnerships forged with staff in the institutional research office, academic and administrative computing services, admissions, and the registrar's office can be critical to meeting student affairs information needs.

Institutional research units often produce an annual fact book or publish periodic reports and research findings containing student demographic information and recruitment and retention data useful for shaping student affairs goals and objectives. The professional staff can also lend technical expertise in selecting research samples, determining data collection methodologies, and refining instruments. Learning in advance about the development of a comprehensive survey and being able to add questions illustrate the benefits of a strong communication link with the institutional research office. However, when it comes to undertaking comprehensive research efforts for student affairs, higher priorities may prevail and the concept of student development and its measurement may not be within the institutional researchers' areas of expertise. Nonetheless, a strong relationship cultivated by a student affairs representative who is an expert in research is needed to ensure that this information-fertile area is maximally used by student affairs.

Through connections with the institution's computing services, student affairs staff can learn about useful reports generated originally for other units, submit requests for developing specialized reports, and gain assistance in scanning surveys or writing programs to tally the results. However, the number of requests received by campus computing services, the location of student affairs jobs in the list of priorities, and the ever-changing state and federal reporting requirements that affect existing computer programs can present real barriers to the fulfillment of student affairs requests on many campuses. On campuses where student affairs units have developed their own technological support, or where staff have gained substantial computer proficiencies, the programming assistance available through centralized computing offices becomes less relevant. Instead, staff members manipulate downloaded mainframe data or access data subsets by using SQL (Structured Query Language) servers to obtain the information needed.

Student affairs staff can share information interests with those in administrative units outside the division (for example, admissions office, registrar's office, and enrollment services if they reside outside the student affairs division). Exchanging data and reports, collaborating on survey designs, and submitting joint requests to institutional research and computing units can all be mutually beneficial.

The range of departments that can assist with student affairs data collection is extensive. Development office facilities designed for telephone fundraising campaigns are useful for conducting program evaluations by phone. Marketing departments may also have the telephone facilities and software for tabulating survey results when entered directly into the computer.

The resources to assist with student affairs data collection are equally vast when looking off-campus. Numerous websites and listservs are available on the Internet, and printed publications regarding student affairs research have grown over the last decade. However, one of the most productive ways to gain research-related insights or information is by communicating with colleagues sharing similar interests who have been identified through conference presentations or the professional literature.

Diverse Data Collection Approaches

Research experience at UTA has shown that both pragmatism and creativity are needed when considering possible data collection approaches. In-class surveys, telephone interviews, mailed surveys, focus groups, suggestion boxes, and database analyses are options commonly considered because of their strengths (for example, ability to obtain responses, opportunity to probe further) or rejected on the basis of their weaknesses (cost, lack of random selection, low returns, respondents' inability to consult others). With a little ingenuity, further alternatives can be uncovered. Campus procedures sometimes provide opportunities, like interviewing students face-to-face while they wait in line or asking questions as part of an automated telephone registration process. Establishing an agreement with a commercial marketing company that collects consumer preferences via stand-alone computers is another option. In this instance, questions of interest to student affairs are included in exchange for providing secure locations for placing the polling devices.

Types of Data Collected

Two decades ago, many student affairs professionals noted with frustration that the results of their work could not be measured. For example, it was felt that due to the myriad factors that affect student recruitment and retention, the impact of student affairs administrators could not be readily determined. This widely communicated declaration caused some practitioners to turn their backs on data collection, judging it to be a futile undertaking. In contrast, others, including UTA, held an unswerving commitment to data collection for planning purposes, personnel and program development, and for the sake of accountability.

Broadly speaking, data collected by UTA's student affairs researchers fall into three broad categories: (1) clientele and user characteristics, (2) program and personnel evaluations, and (3) outcomes data. These categories are presented in the order in which they were phased in and according to methodological complexity.

Clientele and User Characteristics. The initial phase of UTA's Student Affairs data collection effort involved gathering information about the characteristics of the student body and of the users of student affairs programs and services. The key elements include the following.

Counts of Students Served and Contacted by Program Area. For many years, UTA's Student Affairs staff members manually recorded the number of persons served (each user/participant counted only once) and the numbers contacted (individuals may be counted more than once) for each program area. Ethnicity and sex were also recorded. This information is valuable when designing marketing plans and planning pertinent programs, and in budget hearings and in developing program priorities for funding purposes (Moxley and Duke, 1986).

The recent implementation of a campus-wide, computer-readable ID card and the installation of scanners at campus service points have substantially increased the accuracy and the amount of service user information collected at UTA. By matching the ID numbers recorded by the scanners with student demographics in the university's student database, a tremendous amount of planning-related information is gained. A report has been developed that displays the number of users and contacts for selected program areas. The data are displayed by demographic characteristics [for example: sex, ethnicity, classification, school/college affiliation, status (day/night/both, full- and part-time), residency, age, mode of admission] as well as the numbers served each hour. Improved program marketing and better matches between staffing and service activity are among the benefits derived from this computerized approach to counting students.

Database Reports. Over the years, student affairs researchers at UTA prepared reports comparing the characteristics of registered and withdrawn students. These reports have been distributed periodically to all deans, directors, and department heads. The findings help university officials recognize that retention efforts should focus on evening, part-time, and older students. It is also through student affairs database reports that the university was made aware of its graduation rates for first-time freshmen by ethnic group and all groups combined. Many of the student affairs database reports are essential for program administration (for example, the listing of students with grade point averages below 2.5 used for peer advising purposes). Other reports are designed to provide measures of results (for example, course grades for tutored students and the proportion of tutored students who re-enroll and graduate). Finally, some reports influence policy decisions such as the determination of office hours or entrance score requirements. With the development of the Institutional Research and Planning Office, reports pertinent to the university at large now emanate primarily from that unit.

Student Survey. The comprehensive student survey, developed in-house and administered in the classrooms in 1963 and about every five years thereafter, is one of the most useful data collection tools used at UTA. Nearly a third of the student body provides information about their own characteristics (for example, commuting distance, employment status, marital status, reasons for enrolling) and satisfaction with various aspects of the university, such as academic advising, library services, teaching in one's major field, and cultural opportunities. The findings have become an invaluable resource in the university's planning process and have allowed the university to respond more effectively to student needs.

Program and Personnel Evaluations. Program and personnel evaluations form the second order of data collected by the Division.

Program Evaluations. In the early 1980s, student affairs researchers began to work with directors and the vice president to implement periodic program evaluations completed by a random sample of the student body or users of the respective student affairs programs/services. Surveys and related research reports were requested from other institutions to assist with instrument design and to use for data comparisons. Ultimately, the student affairs program evaluation resources were sufficiently large to establish a Student Affairs Research Clearinghouse. For over a decade, the Clearinghouse served an eleven-state area through the support of the National Association of Student Personnel

Administrators Region III and the Texas Association of College and University Student Personnel Administrators.

In addition to the comprehensive evaluations completed by program/ service users, a wide range of specialized evaluations has been implemented within the Student Affairs Division to address specific issues. For instance, differences in user and nonuser perspectives were obtained for the financial aid office, the Student Health Services was particularly interested in the evening students' view of their operating hours, and the faculty's perception of the current and ideal roles of the student activities office provided useful information for that unit. Evaluation results have guided staff development programs and have prompted the introduction, modification, and demise of programs. Most recently, data collected from international and resident students prompted the implementation of a Saturday shopping shuttle and rider evaluations caused modifications in the route.

Personnel Evaluations. In the early 1980s, the division initiated a special form for evaluating the vice president for student affairs (to be completed by division staff) and specific forms for professional staff, directors, and the secretarial/clerical support staff. Several of these forms were later replaced when a university-wide form was developed for annual performance appraisals. However, several job-specific performance appraisal forms, such as those for academic tutors and aerobics instructors, are presently used within the division.

Over the years the vice president has utilized various methods for evaluating directors. One of the most constructive approaches encompasses "bottom-up" reviews. Individuals reporting to a director and the support staff members who share the director's work environment complete an employee satisfaction survey and a form evaluating the director's performance. The division's lead researcher tallies the anonymous surveys and prepares associated reports. Results from these periodic reviews are used for performance improvement discussions between the vice president and the respective directors. In addition, student affairs directors receive program-based reviews when they discuss their annual reports with the vice president for student affairs.

The data collection instruments used by UTA's Student Affairs Division and the associated written reports (excluding personnel appraisals) are found in a series of notebooks labeled *Student Affairs Planning Documents,* which are located in the Office of the Vice President for Student Affairs. These volumes also include departmental annual reports and budgets, organizational charts, and a listing of the actions taken as a result of each research effort. They are consulted regularly for planning purposes and when new instruments are needed.

Outcomes Data. The collection of outcomes data is now the primary research emphasis for UTA's Student Affairs Division. About five years ago the division launched its student development outcomes project. The professional literature lacked a systematic discussion of possible outcomes that student affairs practitioners could affect and alternative means for measuring them. Consequently, a literature search was conducted to identify student development areas influenced by student affairs. Nearly 50 were uncovered, ranging from the development of social responsibilities, academic skills, and cultural appreciation to physical and interpersonal skills development. The student affairs directors collectively clustered the items with common characteristics and ultimately identified eight broad outcome areas: (1) involvement in university life, (2) satisfaction with the university experience, (3) intellectual development (such as aesthetic/cultural appreciation and academic skills), (4) emotional development (such as self-concept, self-esteem, and autonomy), (5) ethical development (such as social responsibility, values development, and integrity), (6) social development (such as leadership, group interaction, and interpersonal development), (7) career development (that is, career decision making and development of purpose), and (8) physical development (for example, physical fitness and development of leisure interests).

In the absence of a compendium regarding possible outcomes and related measuring instruments, the UTA student affairs researchers submitted a grant proposal to the state's professional organization to publish such a document and to distribute it to professionals within the state. The Texas Association of College and University Student Personnel Administrators awarded the funds, and a reference booklet entitled *Student Affairs-Related Outcomes Instruments: Summary Information* (Lewis, Moxley, Stigall, and Dortch, 1994) was produced. UTA's researchers clearly had addressed a need; without any formal advertising, over 400 booklets were purchased within the first year.

With information about published student affairs–related outcomes instruments, UTA's Student Affairs Division implemented several data collection efforts. The *College Student Experience Questionnaire,* developed by Robert Pace at the University of California at Los Angeles, was administered in the classroom. Because it permitted the inclusion of campus-based questions, information was collected concerning all eight developmental areas noted above. American College Testing Program's *College Outcomes Survey* with thirty supplemental questions has been administered in college adjustment and student leadership classes and given to students in leadership positions in a pre- and posttest fashion in an effort to discern the impact of these particular experiences.

Instruments have also been created in-house to measure outcomes. The most recent administration of the university's comprehensive *Student Survey* included an outcomes-related section. Even the division's staff development committee has taken an outcomes-oriented focus to the evaluation of educational programs it sponsors. Pre- and posttest instruments have been administered to division staff as they begin and complete the Noel-Levitz *Advanced Connections* customer service program.

Database studies are equally valuable when examining outcomes. For example, UTA data show that students using the campus tutoring program graduate at a higher rate than nonusers, even though the standardized admissions test score means for the tutored group are significantly below the mean test scores for those not using the tutorial services. Similarly, students mentored within the Student Governance and Organizations mentoring program have higher one-year retention rates than the overall campus average.

The Value of Information Is in Its Use

Not all staff members in the Student Affairs Division are eager to be evaluated, and some may keep the findings hidden in their bottom drawers. Similarly, some executive officers disregard the student affairs information they receive. However, most student affairs directors and staff members, and certainly the vice president, eagerly await the research and evaluation results and study them intently to identify ways that the programs and services can be improved.

Indeed, the effectiveness approach that the division has applied—establishing goals, implementing, evaluating, and making modifications on the basis of information—has produced considerable programmatic change and very positive results. In illustration, information caused Counseling and Career Development to expand its hours and outreach efforts; Multicultural Services implemented a faculty/staff mentoring program for students; a division-wide marketing committee was formed; the International Office developed a shortened transfer student orientation program; the Greek rush schedule changed radically; the tutoring program added more seminar topics and modified its billing system; a comprehensive training program commenced for test proctors; Student Health Services began accepting credit card payments and expanded the pharmacy inventory; MAVMAIL, a speedy information and referral system, was put into place; an information and visitor center was established; the preferred style of housing was used when contracting with external builders; customer service training commenced; the student handbook now includes a planner; and an employee wellness program with release time for participation was implemented (Moxley, 1990). On the whole, the results have been remarkable. The overall grade point average and graduation rates of students using the student affairs tutorial services exceed the university average; students participating in the mentoring program are retained at higher rates than nonparticipants; the Movin' Mav Wheelchair Basketball Team has captured its fifth National Intercollegiate Championship; and *The Shorthorn*, UTA's daily newspaper, was named best college newspaper by both the Texas Intercollegiate Press Association and the Rocky Mountain Collegiate Media Association (RMCMA) competitions, and it has received the Pacemaker Award.

Research indicates that information is the chief student affairs administrator's most important source of power in the budgetary process (Moxley, 1980). The use of information at UTA has greatly affected the division's funding. Historically, the university's financial decision makers found the student affairs researchers' list of ways research findings help the institution monetarily to be quite appealing. For example, evaluation of the food service operation brought changes in the hours, menu mix, and price structures, which were key factors in making a deficit operation fiscally sound. The researchers' review of departmental budgets before the formal budgetary hearings improved the match between the requests and departmental objectives, curbed unrealistic requests, and eliminated budget development errors. Research and evaluation findings are also useful to other student affairs directors in budgetary hearings. This includes evaluation findings that (1) document program results (like improved grade point averages or retention rates), (2) demonstrate student endorsement of the program (for example, Disabled Student Services ranked third out of nineteen areas in the number of students wanting their fees to support it), or (3) indicate a relationship to student goals or needs (such as, 68.8 percent of the in-class survey respondents checked preparing for a job or career as their most important academic goal, and 69.6 percent checked that they needed career counseling).

In times of growing competition for state funds and student fees, it is essential to seek alternative external sources of funds to support student affairs programs and services. UTA's Student Affairs Division readily uses research and evaluation findings to support grant proposals. Over the past several years, the division has attracted well over $1,000,000 in external funds. The division sets the pace for student affairs units on peer campuses and it also compares well with the academic schools and colleges on the UTA campus (typically ranking third, following the College of Engineering and College of Science). For example, research and evaluation findings have helped obtain (1) faculty mentors, stipends, and research experience for talented students from cohorts underrepresented in graduate programs (McNair Scholars Program, U.S. Department of Education); (2) academic counseling and tutoring for qualified students (SOAR-Student Support Services, U.S. Department of Education); (3) a substance abuse prevention program (Student Health Services, U.S. Department of Education); (4) cultural events—ballet, musical, children and adult theatrical productions (Student Activities–Texas Commission of the Arts); and (5) International Week marketing (International Office, Arts and Cultural Grant Program, City of Arlington).

Epilogue

Within a year after UTA's Student Affairs Division received its second commendation from the Southern Association of Colleges and Schools reaccreditation team, the new president dismantled the Student Affairs Division "as part of a reorganization designed to better support the university's academic mission and goals, to increase administrative effectiveness and efficiency, and to reduce central administration staff expenses" (Witt, 1997, p. 1). Student Health Services was placed under the School of Nursing; the University Center now reports to the director of the Physical Plant; campus Housing may be privatized; the Dean of Student's area (including Student Activities, Student Governance and Organizations, Disabled Student Services, Attorney for the Students, Multicultural Services), Counseling and Career Development, Student Employment, several federally sponsored TRIO programs, and Recreational Sports are now found under the former vice provost for academic affairs, who has become the vice president for undergraduate academic and student affairs; and the International Office and the Educational Opportunity Center (one of the TRIO programs) will report to the senior vice president for academic affairs and provost. The vice president who successfully led the Student Affairs Division for twenty-six years has been reassigned to duties that have not yet been clarified, and the assistant vice president (researcher) and executive assistant to the vice president have not yet heard their fates from the president. There are now new opportunities and challenges for conducting student affairs research and evaluations.

References

Commission on Colleges, Southern Association of Colleges and Schools. *Resource Manual on Institutional Effectiveness* (3rd ed.). Decatur, Georgia: Commission on Colleges, Southern Association of Colleges and Schools. 1996.

Commission on Colleges, Southern Association of Colleges and Schools. *Report of the Reaffirmation Committee.* Arlington: The University of Texas at Arlington, February 10–13, 1997.

Ezell, J. B., and others. *Visiting Committee Report.* Arlington: The University of Texas at Arlington, April 22–25, 1986.

Lewis, L. G., Moxley, L. S., Stigall, S., and Dortch, M. F. *Student Affairs-Related Outcomes Instruments: Summary Information.* Arlington: Student Affairs, The University of Texas at Arlington, Spring 1994.

Moxley, L. S. "The Student Personnel Administrator in the Budgetary Process: Decision Structures, Power, and Purse Strings." Unpublished doctoral dissertation, Center for the Study of Higher Education, The University of Michigan, 1980.

Moxley, L. S. "The Role and Impact of a Student Affairs Research and Evaluation Office." *NASPA Journal,* 1988, *25* (3), 174–179.

Moxley, L. S. "The Development and Impact of an Experimental Student Affairs Wellness Program." *Research in Higher Education,* 1990, *31* (3), 211–233.

Moxley, L. S., and Duke, W. "Setting Priorities for Student Affairs Programs for Budgetary Purposes: A Case Study." *NASPA Journal,* 1986, *23*(4), 21–28.

Witt, R. E. "December 1, 1997" (press release). Arlington: President's Office, The University of Texas at Arlington, December 1, 1997.

LINDA S. MOXLEY *is assistant vice president for student affairs at the University of Texas at Arlington.*

This is the fifteen-year story of the student affairs research operation at Northeastern University, covering the initial buildup, the demise due to institutional downsizing, and the resurrection.

Student Opinion Surveys at Northeastern University

Anthony J. Bajdek, Sungwoo Kim

When satisfaction declines or disappears among the voting public with its elected representatives in government, and among consumers with products and services from the corporate sector of American life, the outcomes become readily apparent. In today's world, opinion surveys not only constitute one approach for ensuring effective communication, thereby enhancing quality control as well as gaining the competitive edge, but also, *most important,* they enable consumers to express their opinions about the products and services they purchase directly or receive indirectly by way of taxation.

Opinion surveys are very valuable, yet relatively few colleges and universities engage in student opinion research with or without the involvement of student affairs departments. Perhaps it is because college/university administrators are confident that they possess, through years of practical experience, all the answers to their student-based problems, the most compelling of which today is the much sought after Holy Grail for improved retention. Perhaps they are reluctant to associate the experience of problem solving in higher education with that, for example, of the corporate sector. Perhaps student affairs administrators and their academic colleagues do not view research as an appropriate activity for student affairs professionals. Contemporary higher education *is* a large industry in America; accordingly, students, as well as their parents, exercise their consumer consciousness. This consideration might well become the driving force for a change in thinking about the topic in American higher education.

The Origin of Student Affairs Research at Northeastern

At Northeastern University, we had been fortunate to have an executive vice president, John A. Curry (later becoming the university's fifth president), who strongly endorsed this chapter's opening proposition, particularly as it related to understanding the student perspective about the institutional challenges of attrition and retention. The narrative that follows is essentially a happy story with a sad ending as it developed from 1983 through 1991, to be followed by an interregnum and resurrection in 1997, or stated differently, now you see it, now you don't, now you see it again. It demonstrates that albeit the quality of research and its practical applicability are very important, other external considerations often influence the destiny of sustaining student affairs–related research. It also demonstrates, at least by way of our experience, that a *good idea* (that is, student opinion surveys conducted by student affairs staff alone or in collaboration with individual faculty members or institutional research units) can resurface and find new life.

Our story's foundation actually began in late 1982 when one of us co-authored a longitudinal study of the University's class of 1982 in which the persistence/nonpersistence characteristics of every student were carefully identified (Bajdek and Nachorski, 1983). That study endeavored to identify, among other things, whether persisters differed in their academic performance from their nonpersisting counterparts. Prior to that study, the general perception of many of the university's administrators and faculty had been that nonpersisters were essentially weak, unmotivated students who couldn't measure up. Over 4,000 individual academic records were analyzed by SAT scores, admissions department ranks, gender, college, major field of study, and performance in key courses at the freshman and sophomore levels, which, as was known, were the primary and secondary highest points of attrition at Northeastern as well as elsewhere.

One of the findings showed that nonpersisters differed from persisters only by half a letter grade in course performance. However, though the study identified precise benchmarks related to persisters and nonpersisters in the class of 1982, it could not disclose what the students thought of the undergraduate experience at Northeastern that motivated them to persist or withdraw. This typified the limitations of all longitudinal database studies— the fact that they failed to incorporate the student perspective, thereby limiting considerably a researcher's understanding of the dynamic of attrition/retention, which is, after all, a two-sided phenomenon. The truth about attrition/retention was located somewhere on a plane between *how a university viewed its students,* on one hand, and *how its students viewed the university,* on the other.

It was precisely this reason that subsequently brought us together as a team for more than an eight-year collaboration in student opinion research at Northeastern. Our collaboration was as beneficial for the university as it had been productive for us. We produced fourteen reports, four of which were presented in modified format at various professional conferences [two Noel/Levitz national retention conferences (Kim and Bajdek, 1988a, 1991), one regional NASPA conference (Kim, Bajdek, and Carter, 1989), and one Regional ACAFAD conference (Bajdek, 1988)]. One study was published in the *Social Science Perspective Journal* (Kim, Bajdek, and Bork, 1989), and one later became a chapter in a book (Rhem, 1988).

Critics might argue that our research output over eight years had actually been scanty. The point to remember, however, is that we were not a department, but rather we were concerned employees who *collaborated* for the surveys/reports, the focus of which was the improvement of retention in our university. The team consisted of a professor of economics with research specialization in the economy of Korea, and an associate dean of students and director of the Office of Freshman Affairs, who was also a senior lecturer in the history department. Funding for the research was provided by the executive vice president on an annual basis, subject to our satisfactory performance and the practical applicability of our research.

Surveys of the Undergraduate Experience

After completing two relatively modest preparatory runs in our winter (1984) quarter (on nonpersisters, unsurprisingly) and in November 1986 (persisters) for the benefit of the executive vice president whose approval for funding we sought, we embarked on our most ambitious project in late 1986–early 1987 (Kim and Bajdek, 1987). For this latter study, we randomly selected a sample of 7,000 freshmen through senior year level students from the university's database of 17,083 full-time day undergraduate student population. Our strategy was to achieve two basic objectives. The first objective was to solicit accurately the students' perspectives about their undergraduate experiences by using seventy-two questions grouped into the six major categories that we proposed constituted the undergraduate experience at Northeastern: (1) the quality of teaching, (2) faculty advising, (3) administrative staff counseling, (4) registration, (5) campus facilities and social events, and (6) Co-op work experiences. The second objective was to measure students' opinions by continuous and quantitative units rather than by discreet or qualitative units so as to carry out statistical analysis. In terms of our first objective, we agreed to measure student opinion by a twenty point scoring system, ranging from -10 (extremely dissatisfied) to -1 (marginally dissatisfied), and from $+1$ (marginally satisfied) to $+10$ (extremely satisfied).

When we circulated our proposed four-page questionnaire to university colleagues who had experience with opinion surveys, they expressed two criticisms. First, since students would be asked to respond to the survey on a voluntary basis, most students, they cautioned, would not take the time to answer the survey's seventy-two questions. Second, they speculated that our full-time undergraduate students did not have sufficiently precise opinions about the university experience to answer the questions on a twenty-point basis. Therefore, our colleagues suggested that we employ a much shorter and simpler questionnaire.

However, when we tested the questionnaire on a small sample of students, the results disproved our colleagues' criticisms. We were encouraged to embark on our quest to identify factors of the Northeastern University undergraduate experience that pleased students and encouraged their persistence through the point of graduation. We also chose to identify factors that displeased students and caused them to leave the university. We distributed the questionnaire to our sample in January 1987. Half of the sample was asked to complete the questionnaire on site during the registration process, and the other half received their questionnaires via the mail and were provided with postage-paid, pre-addressed return envelopes.

To our utter surprise and delight, 2,667 students (38 percent of the sample) voluntarily completed the questionnaire. Moreover, 998 of them voluntarily provided us their student identification numbers, thus enabling us to ascertain the truth of their answers (for instance, on QPA—quality point average) as well as to conduct a longitudinal analysis at a later time. As the means by which to test our respondents' honesty in answering the questions, we correlated the average of the self-reported QPAs for 200 randomly selected students from the pool of 998 who volunteered their student identification numbers with their actual QPAs on the university's database. The difference between the former (2.9956) and the latter (2.9530) was only .0426, which was about 1.4 percent of their actual QPAs at the time and a difference much smaller than normal random error on this type of survey. Consequently, we were convinced not only of the sincerity of our respondents but also of the reasonable accuracy of the information derived from our survey in general.

We went on to rank answers to the seventy-two individual questions in descending order in terms of their mathematical averages and standard deviations for respondents as a whole as well as for numerous subgroups (for example, gender, years of graduation, race, colleges, major fields of study). In addition to grouping seventy-one of the questions into the six major categories noted earlier, the seventy-second question was designed for measuring the students' overall satisfaction with the university and served as a dependent variable for multivariate regression analysis with the six major categories.

In terms of averages as well as regressions, our simple analysis revealed several interesting and potentially very important aspects of student opinion at Northeastern that had been hitherto unknown to the administration and faculty. For example, our respondents indicated that although the Co-op program was the most important determinant for selecting Northeastern, once they enrolled, the most important aspect of their undergraduate experience became the quality of teaching, a factor whose importance increased significantly over years as they approached graduation. This challenged our own decades-old institutional stereotype about Co-op, as some would have summarized it, that "Co-op brings them here and Co-op keeps them here." We postulated that if this revelation turned out to be true by other substantiating evidence, the best and most effective policy for improved student retention should be one that improved and sustained high-quality teaching.

Research Serving a Practical Need

Throughout our research, we sought to identify statistically significant dissatisfaction with aspects of the undergraduate experience that fueled attrition. Once accurately identified, the elimination of those particular sources of dissatisfaction would improve students' general satisfaction and concurrently enhance retention. Shortly after releasing the results of our findings to the president, Kenneth G. Ryder, he invited us to present a summary of our findings to his cabinet. One source of dissatisfaction among our respondents concerned the old (Dodge) library, which was by then scheduled to be replaced by a modern, state-of-the-art edifice to be known as the Snell Library. In pointing out to the cabinet that students were dissatisfied with the Dodge Library's insufficient hours of operation, the president immediately responded by ordering that its hours of operation be lengthened, thereby eliminating at least one source of student dissatisfaction.

In our resulting report (Kim and Bajdek, 1988b), we proposed that "once students are well settled into the university after the freshman year, the main determinants for their satisfaction are those factors that students are *constantly* and *significantly* exposed to throughout their school years, and that they tend to forget those factors with which they have to deal only *occasionally*" (p. 19). Our subsequent student opinion research reinforced that proposition. The report, and its associated raw data, would serve as our linchpin for relating data collected from students in future surveys that employed the *same* seventy-two questions but appended additional questions appropriate to the sample being surveyed [for example, nonpersisting as well as persisting students, honors program participants, special support (remedial) program participants, and disabled/deaf and hard-of-hearing students].

The 1989 nonpersisters study, where freshmen and sophomores constituted 89 percent of our respondents, illustrated that the respondents either refused to discuss their decisions to withdraw with any university administrator or faculty member or did not know with whom to discuss their plans to withdraw (Kim and Bajdek, 1989). Nevertheless, the students were *willing* to express their opinions about their undergraduate experiences at Northeastern *after the fact* of their voluntary (as opposed to being withdrawn by action of the university) withdrawals. Moreover, by comparing the satisfaction levels of nonpersisters with those of persisters we were able to identify factors with negative scores that may have contributed to their decisions to leave the university. We found, as expected, that nonpersisters had a much lower level of satisfaction with all individual aspects of the university undergraduate experience than did their persisting fellow students.

As the result of that opinion survey study, we also concluded that the elimination of factors contributing to attrition would also generate goodwill and trust within the student body as it witnesses the university's determination to satisfy their consumer expectations. We were convinced that student retention could become a controllable function if appropriate improvements were made in the university undergraduate experiences that affect the welfare of students *most*. In the university's very urban environment in Boston's Back Bay area, the *constant* and *significant* factor of parking for many of our commuting students further illustrates this point.

When we conducted our survey of persisters in 1987, parking received a serious negative score of −3.62 on our twenty-point scale. In 1990 when we conducted another opinion survey of persisters, the university's new, first-ever parking garage was already in operation, and essentially the same students rated parking with a score of +0.46, an increase of 4.08 points. Improvement in parking may not have necessarily improved the prestige of the university, but it certainly contributed visibly to the welfare of our students, thereby affording them more reasons for completing their baccalaureate educations with us.

Research on Students Participating in Honors Program

Honors program participants are yet another example of the far-reaching practical impact of our student opinion research activities. In 1986–1987, there were only 281 students enrolled in freshman (167 students) and sophomore (114 students) level honors courses (Kim and Bajdek, 1988c). When we conducted our opinion survey among these students at the request of the program's director, we attracted a response from ninety-nine, or 35 percent of them. What we found was that whereas they were most satisfied with the honors program faculty (mean score of +6.03), they were dissatisfied considerably with the availability of honors courses, a matter requiring immediate corrective attention. In another area for concern, we discovered that our ninety-nine honors respondents were quite unhappy, relatively speaking, with the time required to complete registration in person (their mean score was a +0.79 compared with that of +2.49 for persisters). To say the least, the circumstances causing that problem for them were corrected immediately, and since then for the university generally, which now employs an automated telephone registration system.

Insofar as participation in honors courses has never involved a weighted grading system, we were delighted to learn, as was the director of the honors program, that our respondents were rather well satisfied with grading in honors courses (score of +4.11). Our findings disproved an assumption held by some faculty and administrators that students otherwise eligible for the honors program did not participate in it because they feared that participation would result in lower grades. After cross-tabulating their quality point average (QPA) at Northeastern with their secondary school grade point averages (GPA), we found that their QPAs at Northeastern were higher than their secondary school GPAs. When the university-wide honors program began at Northeastern in 1985, relatively few students participated in it. Since then, the program has grown consistently so that in 1997, for example, some 1,350 students actively participated in it out of a smaller full-time day undergraduate student base of 11,387. We like to believe that our opinion survey during the formative years of the program in some small way at least contributed to the program's subsequent growth and success in satisfying and retaining these excellent students.

The Productive Years

The period from late 1988 through 1991 was very productive for us. We issued seven more student opinion research reports and made related presentations at four conferences. During that period, Carol J. Carter was added to our team as coordinator of research in the Division of Student Affairs. One of her specific tasks was to design and introduce a telephone-based capability for conducting student opinion surveys, to be known as *TeleTalk*, which was based on the Project Pulse survey operation at the University of Massachusetts Amherst. *TeleTalk* surveys augmented student opinion research in the Division of Student Affairs and were conducted for nearly two years. They *also* focused on practical matters influencing campus life such as commuter students, cooperative education, and rape on campus. Clearly, all signs appeared to be positive as far as we, the unnamed collaborators for student opinion research, were concerned and pointed to the possibility of student opinion research becoming a permanent aspect of student affairs. We believed that we were on the right track. Moreover, John A. Curry became president of the university during the same period.

What none of us (Bajdek, Carter, Kim) knew at the time, however, was that Northeastern was on the verge of undergoing an unprecedented major retrenchment experience, as was becoming true for many universities in the early 1990s. Forced to reduce its operating budget, the university had to eliminate 175 positions immediately, almost all of which involved full-time administrators and support staff.

In January 1990, we conducted another survey of persisters, this time deliberately reducing the size of our sample, thereby resulting in a response from 509 students (Kim and Bajdek, 1990). With data from two major surveys of persisters we had an opportunity to compare results, thereby enabling us to determine to what extent student opinion on any given question may have changed over the intervening years. For instance, both in 1987 and in 1990, when we compared the relative importance of student satisfaction with the quality of teaching, we found that it declined to its lowest point between the sophomore and middler years, then steadily increased through the junior and senior years. Because of cooperative education at Northeastern, it generally takes five years to earn the bachelor's degree, thus producing an extra class year designation of "middler." Our research substantiated Northeastern University's pattern of greatest attrition that we termed the "middler year letdown" syndrome (Kim and Bajdek, 1990, p. 46). The regression coefficient for satisfaction with the quality of teaching not only illustrated the university's primary and secondary points of highest attrition but also correlated *progressive dissatisfaction* with that factor as the likely significant cause of attrition for the students constituting our sample. In 1990, the university established the Office for the Support of Effective Teaching; in 1996, it was redesignated as the Center for Effective University Teaching. Coincidence or not, we never knew. We make no claims.

The Demise and Rebirth of Student Opinion Research at Northeastern

Our collaborative work in student opinion research was ended shortly after the University was forced to "downsize" in February 1991. Given the atmosphere of crisis that permeated the university at the time, it was a reality that we accepted without protest. We felt good about completing a mission, if you will, that at least demonstrated the usefulness of student opinion research. Fortuitously, one member (Carter) of our three-person team became a successful candidate for a tenured faculty position at another university. We continued to discharge our responsibilities in our respective departments.

In 1995, as the original two founding members of the unnamed student opinion research team in student affairs, we felt obligated to issue a brief closing report to President Curry on the fate of the 998 students who identified themselves in our first major survey of January 1987 (Kim and Bajdek, 1995). We found that the students constituting this sample within a sample, if you will, graduated from Northeastern at a frequency two times higher than the graduation rate of the university as a whole, a point that suggests a great retention intervention strategy!

Between the end of our collaboration and the present, one of us (Bajdek) has conducted occasional student opinion surveys [for example, on the Disability Resource Center (Bajdek, 1997) and on international students (Bajdek, 1992)]. With a financially stronger university and the 1996 arrival of the university's sixth president, Richard M. Freeland, the future involvement of student affairs with student opinion research has been extended the possibility for a new life.

In response to the president's request for the submission of proposals for improving campus life under the President's Intensification Initiatives fund, the vice president of student affairs submitted a proposal for creating a telephone-based student opinion survey system on the model of the University of Massachusetts Amherst's *Project Pulse*. In anticipation of attracting startup funding, Bajdek and the director of institutional research (IR) at Northeastern visited the University of Massachusetts Amherst to seek advice. The IR office and student affairs then collaborated in May 1997 for a pilot demonstration of our proposed *NU PULSE* system, which involved conducting a survey by telephone of a combined sample of 1590 equally divided commuting as well as residential freshmen, of whom 816 responded fully to our questionnaire.

In conclusion, we are pleased to report that on the basis of the pilot's success, President Freeland approved funding for four *NU PULSE* surveys during 1997–1998. In November 1997, we conducted an opinion survey of international students regarding their satisfaction with the services and programs in which they either received or participated. Our second survey in February 1998 sought to identify student satisfaction with the university's varsity sports and intramurals programs. Finally, we are planning to conduct two follow-up surveys of the 816 students who participated in our spring 1998 pilot survey.

Upon learning of President Freeland's approval for funding *NU PULSE*, we were delighted that he stressed that *NU PULSE* opinion surveys must have a practical purpose—to shed light on the university's ongoing challenge for improving retention. That objective reinforces the guiding principle of our earliest student affairs ventures into student opinion research nearly fifteen years ago.

At this point, our narrative ends. If there is a motto to this story, it is "Work hard, keep the faith, and do not complain, because good ideas *do* have a way of resurfacing." Student opinion research is definitely *a good idea,* both for the universities adopting it and for the students whose satisfaction sustains their universities.

References

Bajdek, A. J., "Regularized Student Opinion Surveys: Making a Difference in Higher Education." Paper presented at Northeast Region Conference of the National Association of Academic Affairs Administrators, White Plains, November 4, 1988.

Bajdek, A. J., *Results of the 1991 Survey of Opinion of International Students at Northeastern University.* Boston: Northeastern University, 1992.

Bajdek, A. J., *Evaluation of Services Provided by the Disability Resource Center of Northeastern University.* Boston: Northeastern University, 1997.

Bajdek, A. J., and Nachorski, D. E., *A Longitudinal Analysis of the Class of 1982.* Boston: Northeastern University. 1983.

Kim, S., and Bajdek, A. J., *Results of the 1987 Student Opinion Survey at Northeastern University: Part I, Analysis for the University as a Whole; Part II, Analysis for Individual Colleges; Part III, Analysis for Individual Departments.* Boston: Northeastern University, August, 1987.

Kim, S., and Bajdek, A. J., "What Makes Students Happy: A Regression Analysis of a Recent Student Opinion Survey at Northeastern University." Paper presented at the Noel/Levitz 1988 National Conference on Student Retention, Boston, July 25, 1988a.

Kim, S., and Bajdek, A. J., *Determinants of Student Satisfaction: A Regression Analysis of a Student Opinion Survey at Northeastern University.* Boston: Northeastern University, 1988b.

Kim, S., and Bajdek, A. J., *Analysis of Student Opinion Among Honors Program Participants at Northeastern University.* Boston: Northeastern University, 1988c.

Kim, S., and Bajdek, A. J., *Opinion of Non-Persisting Students at Northeastern University: An Analysis of the 1988–1989 Student Opinion Survey.* Boston: Northeastern University, 1989.

Kim, S., and Bajdek, A. J., *Persisting Students Surveyed in 1990 and 1987: A Comparative Analysis of Student Opinion at Northeastern University.* Boston: Northeastern University, 1990.

Kim, S., and Bajdek, A. J., "Retaining Satisfied Students: Student Opinions Change Over Time—A Case Study." Paper presented at the Noel/Levitz 1991 National Conference on Student Retention, New York, July 30, 1991.

Kim, S., and Bajdek, A. J., *Are Undergraduate Students Who Complete Questionnaires More Likely to Graduate Than Those Who Do Not?* Boston: Northeastern University, 1995.

Kim, S., Bajdek, A. J., and Bork, R. K., "Special Problems of Students with Disabilities or Deafness in Higher Education: An Analysis of a Student Opinion Survey at Northeastern University." *Social Science Perspective Journal,* 4 (3), 1989, 93–124.

Kim, S., Bajdek, A. J., and Carter, C., "Regularized Student Opinion Surveys: A Substantive Approach to Involving and Empowering Students and Improving Retention." Paper presented at the Region I Conference of the National Association of Student Personnel Administrators, Springfield, Mass., November, 1989.

Rhem, J. (ed.), *Making Changes: 27 Strategies from Recruitment and Retention.* Madison, Wisc.: Magna Publications, 1988.

Anthony J. Bajdek is associate dean for administrative services and operations in the division of student affairs at Northeastern University.

Sungwoo Kim is professor of economics at Northeastern University.

*Community college leaders express many ideas pertaining to research
and assessment in student affairs at two-year institutions.*

View from Community Colleges

Gwendolyn Jordan Dungy

The likelihood of finding staff specifically assigned to support research needs of student services areas in community colleges is as probable as winning the lottery or having the team from a magazine sweepstakes contest ring your doorbell after the Super Bowl game in January. When I asked one vice president of student services what she thought about the idea of a research function in student affairs, she said, "That's nuts! We're trying to justify the positions we already have, so it is unrealistic to expect more staff for research." In contrast, Tom Flynn, vice president of student services and administration at Monroe Community College, New York, responded to the same question with, "It is absolutely feasible to have research report to student affairs." He did not limit his thinking to a single staff person in student affairs devoted to research, but thought it feasible that the entire college office of institutional research would be under the supervision of the senior student affairs administrator! To put the idea of research in student affairs in community colleges in context, I first need to describe the current pressures on community colleges and then share how research may be defined in most community colleges.

Generally and ideally, community colleges mirror the personality of their surrounding communities, and collectively they include a growing percentage of the U.S. population pursuing higher education. These colleges belong to the community, and their priority is to address community needs through course offerings and specialized support programs. Community for these two-year colleges includes businesses and corporations that make up the national workforce. Community colleges, perhaps more than any other sector of higher education, are expected to respond to what Theodore Hershberg, professor of public policy and history at the University of Pennsylvania, calls the "human-capital-development challenge." The National Workforce Development Study by the American Association of Community Colleges confirms that "ninety-five percent of businesses and organizations surveyed reported they would recommend community college workforce education and training programs to others" (Zeiss, 1997, p. 51). With such expectations, community colleges are required to create reports that demonstrate their contributions to the success of students and to the larger goal of educating and training workers who will keep the United States competitive.

Though the general public may not be aware that there is a major unit of the college called student affairs or student services, as is more often the title in community colleges, student services has a key role in helping these colleges reach goals of accountability. If students are not applying and attending college, if they are not remaining in college for goal attainment, if they are inadequately prepared for jobs, student services is expected to help provide answers to the question, "Why?"

More and more segments of higher education are responding to pressures from legislators, parents, corporate heads, and students themselves to deliver goods that are judged as practical in helping students get jobs. Corporations are demanding that future employees come to them with basic competencies in reading, computing, communicating, and thinking. Consequently, all units of the college exist to contribute positively to these results. Therefore, whether it is feasible or not to measure a unit's contributions to students' basic competencies, student services in community colleges want indications that their programs and services are effective in helping meet student and workforce needs. Collection of such measurement data falls under the rubric of research.

When community college student services administrators or administrators in offices of institutional research speak about research, they are generally not concerned about the strict definitions of research methodology. The best-case scenario will feature a research design whereby data are collected on those students who participate in particular programs and use specific services under review. Seldom is it possible to develop experimental designs that include control and experimental groups, because community college students are generally fitting classes in between responsibilities at work and home. Perhaps the best circumstances, in the absence of control groups and experimental groups, are pre- and posttest designs for research.

With relevance high on the agenda and time a major factor, any data systematically collected that provides practical information for decision making is defined as "research." For example, the offices of institutional research (IR) provide numerically descriptive snapshots as well as broad overviews of the college. They support planning and evaluation and provide information and data for accreditation, mandatory state and federal reports, and, of course, on enrollment and graduation rates. Generally, they see themselves primarily as "number crunchers" in service to the president and the president's cabinet. They say what they do is to provide "research" data for, on, and about the institution.

Student services administrators say what they want is some form of research or assessment to provide documentation on services and a better understanding of processes and outcomes to improve programs such as orientation and academic advising. Research is often heuristic but accepted as evidence to support current processes or to make a change in procedures. Though analysis and interpretation of the data may not fit the strict definitions of scientific research, this quantifiable and systematically collected information is no less useful in providing direction and information for decision making.

Community college administrators are relatively secure in these practices of data collection and uses because the results address fundamental questions. However, some say they need more empirically based research with true experimental designs to give them a better understanding of some of their perennial problems.

Harry Harden, dean of student development at Montgomery College in Germantown, Maryland, who worked at the Catholic University of America before coming to the community college, said, "At Catholic University, research was pretty much expected, and it was done by professionals working in student affairs. It was routine and ongoing." He thinks research is less of an expectation in community colleges—less of an expectation, perhaps, but a great need according to administrators in student affairs. Expectations, needs, and means are interconnected variables in promoting the idea of a research role and function in student services in community colleges.

Administrators at community colleges today express the same reasons for wanting more research as Linda Moxley (1988) talks about regarding what prompted the University of Texas at Arlington to create one of the few research and evaluation offices for student affairs. The need to make decisions on the basis of facts, the demand for accountability, and a desire to use the division's (and institution's) resources and personal talents wisely, still top the list. Many of these decisions are about the effectiveness of programs and services, and an appropriate balance of costs and benefits of the student services area. Therefore, it is important to realize that the scarcity of research functions in student services does not imply the lack of need for research (Moxley, 1988).

The Need for More Research on Students

Guess Who's Coming to Dinner is a classic film made in 1967 in which Sidney Poitier plays a research physician who is black, and is introduced to the white family of his fiancée. Thirty years ago, this situation was novel enough to serve as the controlling theme for a major film. Just as the film would stir little interest today, the idea of changing demographics on college campuses is hardly news to anyone. What is news is that new students often require new and different programs, and nowhere is the challenge more acute than in community colleges with their enhanced role of serving the greater number and variety of students attending.

Those who previously had barely acknowledged the existence of community colleges soon realized the potential for their enhanced role when President Clinton in 1997 made access to K–14 education a universal expectation with his new tax credit plans. The focus on community colleges as an option for all who seek learning beyond high school makes attaining the associate degree potentially as traditional as the high school diploma has been over the last century. Community colleges will hold a central and pivotal location between K–12 and four-year colleges and universities. Serving as a gateway for so many students, community colleges are compelled to study who their students are and to identify barriers between these new students and their ultimate success.

Student Characteristics and Attrition. Characteristics of community college students and their experiences range from one end of the demographic continuum to the other. For instance, at the numerous campuses of the Maricopa Community College District in the Phoenix area, the average age of students is thirty years, and 78 percent attend part-time. Many of these students are referred to as returning students, meaning that they may or may not have attended this college or another, but they are returning to the life of a student even if their last educational experience was as a high school student. Such students bring different experiences, skills, expectations, obligations, and privileges with them. Although many want to enter the workforce upon completing the associate degree, one out of four indicated in 1989–1990 that they planned to transfer to a four-year college or university (McCormick, 1997).

Retention of students is a perennial pursuit among student affairs administrators. The attrition rate has been high in community colleges, and they have called the "open door" the "revolving door" on occasion. Administrators often report frustration because they have not determined how to increase the retention of historically underrepresented students in any consistent manner. Research is needed to determine how to stem the flood of leavers.

Though many students in the traditional eighteen- to twenty-year age group attend community colleges to receive their first two years of general education more economically before going on to a four-year college or university, others see attending the community college as an extraordinary opportunity to better their circumstances. To them, it is often a leap ahead, a great escape, the key to the good life. With such life-changing incentives for attending and completing college, administrators and staff are often baffled by the number stopping out and leaving.

Student services staff believe that many of these students often have experiences and circumstances that delay them and cause deleterious effects on their academic achievement in comparison to students who have had the advantage of continuous, successful study. More often than not, students come to community colleges as the first in their families to attend college and often have the additional burden of being among the historically defined minorities.

Minority Students. With increasing numbers of first-generation and minority students beginning their education at community colleges, there is a need for research on who these students are, what they want, and how best to help them close the gap between their potential and eventual success as they define it. New students call for close observation and study to best meet their needs.

Community college administrators need to know why one group of students has a higher attrition rate than others. When there are small groups of students of color, the loss of these students has a profound effect on campus diversity. Further, college attrition affects not only the lives of these students but the health of the economy, with its dependence on qualified workers.

To open doors for students formerly excluded without special attention to their needs is a counterfeit invitation. The new student is in direct contrast to traditional college students for whom programs were originally developed. The new student is radically different from any previous generation, and this shift represents the nation's move toward more adequately realizing the promise of democracy.

In recognition of such a phenomenon, Lanham (1992) sees a "radical democratization of higher learning. . . . In the early nineteenth century only one or two in a hundred Americans attended college, and they were almost all male, white, leisure class native English speakers . . . now half do, and they are often none of these. . . . American minorities hitherto excluded from higher education have demanded access to it, and a new flux of immigrants have joined them" (Lanham, 1992, p. 34).

Students are seeking a chance at a better life through community colleges, and they bring extra baggage that includes poverty. Poverty has and will have a mediating effect on the education of all students. Students who bring both poverty and minority status to the higher education environment need to be listened to in order to be provided appropriate support for academic success.

The statistics on the level of poverty of African-American students attending community colleges are important to consider. Volume I of the *African American Education Data Book* illustrates the barriers attributed to poverty: "43.4 percent of African Americans compared with only 18.2 percent of whites had family incomes below $20,000 . . . 64.9 percent of African-American men and 60.4 percent of African-American women were in households in the bottom half of American socioeconomic status, compared with 46.6 percent of white women and 32.4 percent of white men" (Nettles and Perna, 1997, pp. 197–199).

Community colleges are the first option for many African-American students who fit the economic profile above. The first year is the most common time for all students to stop out or drop out of college, but for African Americans the rate of leaving during the first year is 69.8 percent compared with 60.1 percent of white students. This situation supports the notion that research in community colleges should focus on who is coming to college and what is needed to help them reach their goals.

Spencer (1985) suggests that students of color tend to "read the environment," and an awareness of negativity toward them along with inadequate academic preparation, in some cases, appears to be a threat to the students' ego and self-esteem. Removing themselves from the environment by dropping out, what Spencer calls "short-term solutions," may be their way of maintaining a healthy ego. This hypothesis and others need more study and exploration to address the drop-out rate of students who attend community colleges as their first and most accessible route to higher education. Community colleges should be expected to study this issue and pose solutions.

Understanding Today's Students. In addition to students who begin with academic disadvantages, there is the generational change in attitudes, needs, notions, and perspectives of all students. In a special segment of the *Today Show* in August 1997, we were told that 40 percent of all college students are "returning students" and a thirty-three-year-old woman is the average college student today. There are also differences in what we have known as traditional-age college students. Each generation brings students shaped by experiences different from those who came before. These experiences have a profound impact on students' motivations and capacities to pursue higher education. To assume that programs and services that were adequate for previous students are effective for today's students is to ignore the obvious and deny reality. All of this translates into issues for recruitment and retention for student services.

Student affairs has been in the forefront in acknowledging the changing nature of students. Since admissions offices generally report to student services in community colleges, the student services administrator probably has the most up-to-date information on who students are in the aggregate. Admissions offices track trends and note major shifts in attitudes and values among entering students. The downside of this knowledge of student trends is that student affairs and admissions offices, in particular, have been criticized for catering to consumer-like demands of students during the recruitment process.

Edmundson (1997) most likely expressed the sentiments of many faculty when he wrote that the university was "looking more and more like a retirement spread for the young. Our funds go to construction, into new dorms, into renovating the student union" (p. 43). He says that he must concede that "the consumer ethos is winning" (p. 48). His remedy was to jettison services and just provide essential classroom teaching. He was opposed to responding to students as though they were customers. Edmundson's frustration was palpable. However, it should be understandable that if student services has major responsibilities for recruitment and retention, they must look to the needs of the student market. Here is where we may see a clash of values between some faculty and student services administrators.

Rather than eschew and ignore student consumerism and deny that these attitudes exist, student services in community colleges are balancing two primary roles. On the one hand, they must reinforce academic programs for increased student learning through programming such as service learning, student activities, counseling and advising, and on the other hand, they must provide the kinds of services consumer-oriented students demand.

Without the continuous collection, analysis, and use of data about students, it will not be possible for student services to do their job. The role of student services is to understand student needs and when possible, within the mission of the institution, be responsive.

In addition to acknowledging a market culture among students, the academic atmosphere is suffused with a race toward national educational standards and universal outcomes assessment. Call it research or the collection of data on what we do and what difference it makes, these processes are an expectation from all constituencies, especially accrediting bodies and funders. Whether in a four-year college or university, two-year or community college, independent or public, rural or urban, the need for research on students in relation to educational goals and processes is crucial.

Need for Data on How Programs and Services Promote Student Success

Having a positive impact on retaining students is a cornerstone of the work of student affairs. Some innovations such as "one-stop shopping" were implemented in community colleges more than a decade ago. Such a model is still widely used, but administrators must continue to demonstrate to all constituencies that the change to such a process is worth the resources and efforts.

This idea was addressed in 1984 when the dean of student services at Williamsport Area Community College in Williamsport, Pennsylvania, led an innovation called the Advisement Center Project to deal with retention (Martin, 1987). This became known as the "one-stop shopping" model because they combined all the processes for assessment, registration, and orientation.

In addition to addressing retention, a major objective of the Williamsport project was to increase the "market share" of students who enrolled from their service area. A measure of the worth of the project was developed that noted the number of students who took advantage of the combined services, and compared the numbers of students who applied and actually enrolled over the previous five years with the numbers from the project year.

Another objective of the project was to increase sales of the college's meal plan. With implementation of the project, meal plan enrollment increased nearly 50 percent in volume and revenue.

In addition to reviewing positive results related to objectives, data were collected on student satisfaction and how faculty and staff evaluated the process. Based on positive results of those aspects of the project, the model was adopted with plans to measure the effects on retention at a future date.

Some may argue that the processes described above do not constitute research. But for Williamsport, the data collected served the administrators' needs in making the decision to continue the process. Empirical data on programs in student services are useful and seen as research in community colleges.

Today, according to Paul Raverta, vice president of student services at Holyoke Community College in Massachusetts, community colleges continue to search for "proactive approaches to improve student success and retention." Raverta says that his college established a one-stop model for admissions, assessment, and placement of students, and the change streamlined the enrollment process and also identified high-risk students that staff could respond to prior to the start of classes.

Perhaps the major difference between this "one-stop shopping" model and the Williamsport model is the use of technology. Holyoke has computerized assessment in basic skills and has computerized a student needs inventory. The data become part of the student's educational plan and are available to both faculty and student services. Essentially, the college is collecting data for use in meeting student needs based on information provided by the students. Raverta says, "No longer do our student development programs use a scatter-shot approach to outreach. They focus services on students whose profiles indicate that services would be welcome and effective." Data collected not only indicate areas of greatest needs for students, it also revealed that students were 50 percent more forthcoming in expressing their needs on the electronic instrument than they had been previously on the paper and pencil model. With a belief that identifying needs and providing responsive and convenient services leads to retention, the data collected and analyzed are useful research.

As ubiquitous as the idea of one-stop shopping is today, student services must continue to demonstrate the effectiveness of the process on individual campuses. The need for research in student services in community colleges is continuous even on processes generally accepted as effective.

Bette Simmons, vice president for student services at County College of Morris, New Jersey, says research needs to be conducted not only by community colleges but conducted and shared among all colleges and universities on the issues of ethics and efficacy of on-line counseling, especially regarding confidentiality. Simmons is asking for systematic monitoring and data collection and analysis on whether the effects of the new technological medium enhances, detracts from, or has no effect on the effectiveness of the service.

Although some administrators, such as Simmons, identify specific projects to assess or study, Tom Flynn, vice president of student services and administration at Monroe Community College in New York, says that the greatest needs for research in student services are standard and should be ongoing. They fit within three broad categories, according to Flynn: (1) data on the greater community for workforce development needs, (2) what student services say they do and what they actually do, and (3) measurement of the success of graduates. Whether the needs for data are specific to an identified problem or ongoing, there are special requirements for research on programs and services in student services in community colleges.

Focus and Goals of Research in Community Colleges

Since all colleges and universities share the mission of enabling the acquisition of higher learning skills and knowledge, one would assume some basic foci and goals for research in higher education even though the type of institution does influence the mission.

William Knight, director of institutional research, Bowling Green State University, Bowling Green, Ohio, was asked whether he saw any differences in research goals for two- and four-year institutions, and he suggested that research in two-year colleges may tend to focus more on the needs of the job market, student tracking, and how the institution contributes to economic development. He thought that community colleges would be more aware of the importance of costs and competition for students. He understood that students in community colleges are more likely to be enrolled "sporadically" and that there would be a need to find out how much time stopping-out students took between terms and what they were doing when they were not in attendance.

For four-year colleges, he thought the research focus would be on retention rates and the amount of time it took students to get the degree, as well as faculty productivity and the whole issue of how much time is spent on research as opposed to teaching. Knight's views reflect a broad-brush description of the focus of research at community colleges as different from that at four-year institutions. However, two-year college administrators will want to add retention to the list of priorities, and those in four-year colleges will add costs and competitiveness to their list of priorities, especially those in small liberal arts colleges.

Randall Hickman, director of planning and research at Piedmont Community College, North Carolina, sees the purpose of research at community colleges as one of supporting institutional development and training efforts. He says that the major focus is on tracking the relationship between skills provided by the institution and skills required by the job market, thus confirming the conventional view of the major function of community colleges. He also says that it is important to survey graduates to determine institutional effectiveness. He sees various units within the college as internal clients who need assistance in determining the effectiveness of programs, which includes student satisfaction. However, he said that realistically the primary purpose of the research office is to provide information to state governmental and accrediting agencies.

For Arlene Blaylock in the Office of Institutional Research at Montgomery College, Rockville, Maryland, what is more important than the differences between the foci of research at community and four-year colleges is what actually is being done in research offices in community colleges and what could be done. She says that community colleges tend to do more descriptive studies than research; essentially, demographic data are collected and summarized for reporting. She thinks that this is not enough research to make credible inferences.

Although the data currently collected are useful for student services, Blaylock believes that we need to know not just who is dropping out and for how long, but why students are leaving. In addition, beyond training to meet needs of the workforce, what do students need to complete courses successfully and to acquire other important career skills, such as working in teams and taking leadership responsibilities?

Harry Harden, dean of student development at Montgomery College, Germantown, Maryland, says that he wants data to help him understand possible causal relationships between programs and student success. Harden says that one research focus of the community college ought to be on the effectiveness of assessment tests in placing students when SAT and ACT scores are not used for acceptance. In other words, put first things first: Academic programs to meet job market needs are irrelevant if students are not adequately prepared or supported to pass their academic courses. The one question that rings true for all offices of student affairs, regardless of the sector of higher education, is, What impact does what we do have on student achievement and personal growth? Community college administrators ask questions that cannot be answered without research. For example, do students who participate in student activities programs, clubs, and organizations perform differently academically than students who do not participate? If so, what may be some of the reasons? What impact does use of the career center, counseling services, and advisement have on students? Harden wants to know what longitudinal studies might reveal about the grade point averages of students who begin their college course work in remedial courses in comparison with students who did not take remedial courses. In addition to the study of these kinds of questions, whose answers would have a direct impact on students, Harden would also like to know what services are used most and what services are underutilized.

Although the use of resources must be included in any analysis of services, John Barker, coordinator of institutional research at Oklahoma City Community College, says, "Studying the effects of programs is essential and more important than other data generated by institutional research."

Data collection in community colleges reveals a panoply of approaches to institutional research. Paul Raverta, vice president of student services at Holyoke Community College, Massachusetts, says he is comfortable with the research currently generated by student services and by the office of institutional research. In addition to data from admissions, which is part of student services, the student services unit does annual surveys and conducts focus groups, at minimum, on all programs and services for planning and evaluation. They often use benchmarks to compare their services with other institutions for additional information on how well they are doing with the resources they have.

Raverta cautions student affairs administrators about their zeal to connect their programs and services directly to student learning outcomes. Student learning is a collective goal of the entire institution, and what is measurable is efficiency of services and student satisfaction. Raverta thinks using national standards from professional associations, listening to students, and monitoring processes is how student affairs can best demonstrate effectiveness. Raverta's comments about listening to students is crucial when we think about the changes in the composition of the student body, especially at community colleges.

As vital as the work of student affairs is to the academic environment, students come to college expecting to learn from classroom faculty. The faculty members hold the keys to graduation, which opens doors of opportunity. It stands to reason that students who bring different experiences to college, borne out of poverty in many instances, will need to be taught by faculty who have skills beyond their knowledge of course content. One way student affairs can contribute to student learning is through collaboration with faculty on how best to teach students who must begin their course work through remediation. Together they can identify the faculty competencies that have the most positive impact on student learning. Previous studies have found that many of these competencies are the skills student affairs professionals regularly use in their work, such as listening and facilitation skills. More research in this area would contribute directly to the support of students in their course work. Whether looking at what we do and how we do it, counting the number of students who use services, or identifying competencies for effective teaching, the goal is increased understanding for greater effectiveness.

Practical Implications of Research in Student Affairs

Practical is the operative word here. Little doubt exists about the need for research on students to identify what is necessary to support their success at community colleges. Opinions of student affairs administrators about the feasibility of having a research function in the division vary from thinking it is a crazy idea to thinking that it is not only a good idea but feasible. Nonetheless, when faced with the question of whether to use the resources for a research function in student affairs or add another staff person for direct services, the votes go with the latter.

In addition to the financial improbability of support for a research function solely for student affairs, current staff members often lack the time, expertise, and experience in performing research work. Community college administrators in student services suggest that the best alternative is to insist upon a direct relationship between student affairs and collegewide institutional research. To avoid "research" that is simply the manipulation of data already collected by institutional research, a strong organizational tie between the two areas is necessary.

When administrators in institutional research thought about the practical implications of a research function in student affairs, they expressed perceptions of differences in the orientation to research between student affairs professionals and IR personnel. They describe IR personnel as being numbers-oriented with a focus on student characteristics as data for reporting. They assumed the research focus by student affairs staff would be more student-oriented because they were closer to the daily issues facing students. Though IR people agree that more research is needed to support student affairs, they are not comfortable with the idea of student affairs folks actually doing the research and producing reports.

For example, John Barker, of Oklahoma City Community College, said, "If student affairs had their own research function, competition might arise between the offices because IR offices are territorial and want to control the quality of campus research." He went on to say that it was doubtful that college presidents would see the information generated by student affairs as institutional data and would probably not support wide dissemination of the reports. All IR personnel did agree that a real benefit of student affairs staff doing their own research was that if they generated the information, they would be more likely to use it. IR personnel also admitted that most of the requests for specific research came from student affairs, although those requests were never treated as priorities. It was suggested that the best solution would be hiring one staff person designated to do research for student affairs and one for academic affairs. The advantage here would be the support of other researchers and the aura of credibility.

The consensus among IR personnel and administrators in community colleges is that short of the ideal, the best advice for student affairs is to establish a good relationship with IR. Working with IR at the conceptual level of a project and allowing IR to interact with the computer staff to generate the raw data can develop this relationship. IR folks want their clients to have faith that what they produce is correct and will meet their needs. All agree that mutual confidence comes with time and experiences of working together.

Attempts to link activities and treatments to educational outcomes are laudable, expected, and necessary for community colleges in today's climate of measuring effectiveness and efficiency. But studying outcomes of education on students from the narrow perspective of academic or student affairs will be minimally useful. If student affairs had a research function, the focus would have to be the impact of the entire institution as well as other influences, including what students bring with them. Ultimately, research in community colleges addresses a larger picture of accountability and effectiveness than the student services area alone. Without abundant, reliable, and consistent collection of data on students, programs, and services, policies will be developed and curricula will be created or dismantled based on hunches and varying kinds of unsubstantiated logic.

Conclusion

In the best of all possible worlds, student affairs units would have resources to do research by student affairs professionals trained in research methodology. They would produce reports on students that would be powerful tools for all units of the college. Student affairs would not only share results of their research, they would act on their findings.

In the absence of this possibility, perhaps there are two ways student affairs can be more involved in research at this stage of development. One of these would be to see more decentralization of research across the institution whereby individual units take on some responsibility, with IR serving in a coordinating role to address the questions of quality control and support for individual researchers. This is done now on an ad hoc basis in many colleges and universities. Another way to begin to develop a research function in the community college might be to look to the research program in student services in a nearby research university. Staff and resources of the university might cooperate with the community college on mutual priorities such as the student transfer function.

I am optimistic about the future of research in student affairs in community colleges because of pressures to respond to demands for accountability and the verification of institutional outcomes. As the workload of institutional research offices expands to meet increased demands for mandatory reporting to external agencies, there will be the need to find ways to address substantive issues about programs and services. Readily accessible, reliable information available to the institution would spur the improvement of programs for our changing cohorts of students.

References

Edmundson, M. "On the Uses of a Liberal Education: I. As Lite Entertainment for Bored College Students." *Harper's*, 1997, *295* (1768), 39–50.

Lanham, R. A. "The Extraordinary Convergence: Democracy, Technology, Theory, and the University Curriculum." In D. J. Gless (ed.), *The Politics of Liberal Education*. Durham, N.C.: Duke University Press, 1992.

Martin, W. J. "New Student Intake: A Retention Model for Community Colleges." *NASPA Journal*, 1987, *24* (4), 12–22.

McCormick, A. C., MPR Associates, Inc. *Transfer Behavior Among Beginning Postsecondary Students: 1989–94*. Washington, D.C.: National Center for Education Statistics, 97–266, June 1997.

Moxley, L. "The Role and Impact of a Student Affairs Research Evaluation Office." *NASPA Journal*, 1988, *25* (3), 174–179.

Nettles, M. T., and Perna, L. W. *African-American Education Data Book*. Fairfax, Va.: Frederick D. Patterson Research Institute of the College Fund/UNCF, 1997.

Spencer, M. B. "Racial Variations in Achievement Prediction: The School as Conduit for Macrostructural Cultural Tension." In H. P. McAdoo and J. L. McAdoo (eds.), *Black Children—Social, Educational and Parental Environments*. Newbury Park, Calif.: Sage, 1985.

Zeiss, T. (ed.). *Developing the World's Best Workforce: An Agenda for America's Community Colleges*. Washington, D.C.: American Association of Community Colleges, 1997.

GWENDOLYN JORDAN DUNGY is the executive director of the National Association of Student Personnel Administrators (NASPA).

This chapter examines research related to policy analysis in general and scholarship award policy in particular.

Policy Analysis Research: A New Role for Student Affairs Research

Gary R. Hanson

Policy analysis research is the design, collection, analysis, and dissemination of data or information for the purpose of creating or modifying educational policy. Although many of the techniques and methodologies of traditional educational research are used in policy analysis research, the goals and purposes for doing the research, the timing of the data collection, and the manner in which the results are used may be very different. The purpose of this chapter is to explain why student affairs researchers and administrators should learn how to conduct policy analysis research, define its unique characteristics, identify the basic steps in conducting policy analysis research, and illustrate an example of such a project.

Why Policy Analysis Research?

Student affairs professionals are actively engaged in policy decisions nearly every day. We create policy, implement it, and change it but rarely do we take the time to "evaluate" it. We change admissions standards, create new scholarship award criteria, invoke existing student discipline standards, and establish students' rights and responsibilities for community behavior, just to mention a few such decisions. As student affairs professionals, we also work with our faculty colleagues to establish educational policy and academic standards, review departmental curriculum policies for graduation requirements, and determine scholastic dishonesty policies and procedures. Traditionally, most of our policy action is based on good intentions, common sense, and much heated debate; only rarely do we conduct policy analysis research that leads to well-informed policy decisions. How many times as a student affairs administrator have we implemented a new policy and ended the day with a silent prayer that we did the "right" thing. Policy analysis research helps us make the right decisions, do the "right" things, and sleep better at night!

The primary purpose for conducting policy analysis research is to improve the quality of our educational policy. Institutions are judged by the quality of their policies. Good educational policy enhances the quality of a student's collegiate experience, permits the college or university to function effectively and efficiently, and generally improves the institution's reputation among external constituents. When institutions make uninformed or poor policy decisions, students become frustrated and angry; more time, effort, and money are spent "correcting" misunderstandings; and the mission of the institution is not realized. Policy analysis research provides a way not only to judge the quality of our existing policy but to improve it.

Defining Characteristics of Policy Analysis Research

Policy analysis research can be distinguished from traditional student affairs educational research in six ways. First, the focus of policy analysis research is on policy, not on evaluating programmatic efforts. Rather, the focus is on a specific policy. Policy analysis research should answer questions about the effects of the policy on students and how well implementation of the policy reflects the mission and goal of the institution. In this sense, policy analysis research is like evaluative research, but the focus is on policy and not programs.

Second, the purpose of policy analysis research is to clarify or evaluate the worth of an educational policy. The results are used to "enlighten" decision makers about how well a policy has been implemented, whether the policy is producing the desired consequences, and whether the policy needs to be modified as a result of a change in the initial set of circumstances, environment, or conditions under which the policy was originally developed. The results of policy research also can be used to judge or evaluate the effectiveness of an existing policy. Is the policy producing better results than not having a policy at all? Does the policy work equally well for all the target populations for which it was intended? If we change the policy, what will be the impact on future generations of students? The end product of policy analysis research is an evaluative judgment about the worth of the policy.

Third, policy analysis research routinely involves "data simulations" under varying circumstances or conditions of policy implementation. This feature, more than any other, distinguishes policy analysis research from other traditional forms of educational research. Databases are constructed to conduct the simulation. The policy is "applied" to a particular group of students under a set of "simulated" conditions or circumstances, and the possible outcomes of this implementation are examined. The database can be "queried" multiple times, representing varying conditions, populations, and circumstances, and the consequences of such a policy implementation can be captured. A few examples may illustrate this distinguishing feature of policy simulation. For example, what are the consequences for students' academic performance if we increase the number of freshmen in our residence halls at the expense of asking sophomores, juniors, and seniors to live off-campus? How many students will lose their scholarships if we raise the criteria for keeping them from a cumulative grade point average of 3.00 to 3.25? If we raise the admission standards for our institution, what will be the impact on the diversity of our student population? All of these questions involve policy and all of them can be simulated ahead of time to examine the possible educational outcomes.

A fourth distinguishing feature of policy analysis research is an emphasis on the "projection of outcomes." Policy analysis research not only provides a way to examine the historical trends behind a given educational policy, but also provides a way to use these historical trends to project the consequences and outcomes of the policy to new student populations with new sets of conditions. Consequently, policy analysis research provides a powerful tool for anticipating organizational change and a way to examine new strategies for dealing with it. Policy analysis research must deal necessarily with longitudinal trend data.

A fifth feature of policy analysis research is an emphasis on variability rather than control. Traditional research methodology and design focus on controlling the conditions that might influence the outcome. Policy action research does the opposite. The simulation of policy demands that the conditions as well as the target populations be varied from one simulation to the next, and the impact of those "manipulations" evaluated in terms of the consequential outcomes of the simulated changes in a given policy. By varying the conditions or population of students under consideration, a better understanding of the policy's impact is gained.

A sixth distinguishing feature is that policy analysis research may require that the analyses be conducted on the entire population of students rather than sampling smaller subsets of students. The complexity, breadth, and scope of the policy dictates the appropriate sampling methodology, but more likely than not, the policy analysis research will be based on very large populations of students rather than the small statistical samples typically used with inferential statistics and the more traditional educational research designs. Be prepared to develop large, complex databases on large numbers of students from your institution.

Basic Steps in Conducting Policy Analysis Research

There are five steps in conducting policy analysis research. First, the policy decision maker(s) must be identified and the goals and purposes of the policy analysis research must be outlined, clarified, and agreed upon. In working with the primary decision maker(s), the specific policy must be identified and the purposes of the analyses should be defined in sufficient detail to allow a clear recognition of the finished product. Because the analysis may involve numerous iterations of one or more policy simulations, one of the most difficult aspects of policy analysis research is knowing when the analysis is completed.

Agreement about and identification of the finished product will aid the decision maker(s) and the policy research analyst in bringing the analysis to a close.

Second, data elements that compose the working database must be identified and the source file(s) from which they are derived must be located. These data elements must not only define the "who should be included?" question, but must also define the policy parameters regarding the "when" or time frame of the policy analysis, the "what" of the policy content, and the "how" of the policy implementation. Most policy analysis research demands that data elements from multiple source files be compiled into a working data analysis file before the policy analysis may begin. For example, the data elements defining the "who" issue may require input data such as demographic information about gender, class, ethnicity, and age; process data such as the involvement levels in housing, orientation, retention, or scholarship programs; and outcome data such as academic performance, retention or graduation rates, and satisfaction with services indicators. In addition, the policy analysis files may require that these data be collected over key longitudinal status check points for each individual for which the policy implications are being considered. To develop projections for some policy implications that span multiple semesters or years, trend data for three, five, and ten years may be needed. Finally, data and information about the organizational context in which the particular policy is embedded are needed, particularly if the decision maker wants to monitor the influence of a changing organizational context on the implementation and effectiveness of the policy. Once the data elements are defined, the database(s) may be constructed and prepared for the appropriate analyses.

The third step in conducting any policy analysis research project is to identify the appropriate statistical analysis techniques. Like any traditional educational research project, the choice of analysis tools depends on the underlying form of the data and the specific questions raised. With policy analysis, the most important policy decisions focus on what happens to students over their college careers. The statistical methods selected must provide a way to analyze the impact of policy on students' lives over the entire duration of their college careers. These statistical techniques may vary from simple exploratory data analysis suggested by Tukey (1977) to the more sophisticated techniques of cohort survival analysis, multivariate categorical modeling, and multiple dimensional classification analysis. Most often this stage of the analysis is used to document how the current policy works among past or current populations of students. The next stage will involve the simulation of future applications of the policy to different populations of students or under different sets of criteria for implementing the policy.

The fourth step in policy analysis provides an opportunity to conduct policy simulations—the application of new policy standards or criteria to either an existing or new population of students. Once the database is created, the policy research analyst must work closely, often on a daily basis, with the policy decision maker to identify the manner in which the policy manipulations are defined, implemented in the analysis, and interpreted at the end point of each simulation. New standards may be defined, new student populations may be identified for possible policy implementation, and the worthiness of the outcomes must be evaluated before the next round of simulation can be defined and implemented. The number of iterations required to simulate the application of a given policy is a function of how well the "new" policy being simulated achieves the desired outcome or end product in the mind of the policy decision maker(s). A few or a very large number of simulation analyses may be required. For example, to determine whether changing the admissions policy to raise the admissions test score would have a negative effect on the numbers of minority students admitted to a particular college, the policy could be simulated by examining a previous class of entering students and calculating the number of students, by ethnicity, who "would have been" excluded by the new policy. By running several iterations that set the admissions test score cutoff range at a different point each time, the number of students admitted or denied to the college can be determined. There may be a point at which the goal of increasing the preparation level of the students, as indicated by the admissions test score, could be balanced with the goal of maintaining or improving the ethnic diversity of the "next" entering class. At a minimum, the consequences of the policy simulation could be estimated before having to implement the policy.

The fifth step involves the "validation" of the policy analysis decision. If the purpose of the policy analysis was to set new guidelines for an "old" policy or to establish totally new policy, the evaluation of the policy's worth must be judged. Although the simulations provided a "sneak preview" of the possible policy outcomes, the final judgment must wait until the policy has been implemented and sufficient time has elapsed for the consequences of the new policy to be assessed. An additional assessment of the outcome indicators for a particular population of students to which the policy was applied must be done. If the standards by which the policy outcomes are to be judged are well defined before the policy is implemented, the evaluation will be relatively straightforward and easy. If indicators of how the policy was implemented are assessed and monitored, even better judgments may be made and future improvements and policy simulations conducted to fine-tune the policy.

A Policy Analysis Research Case Study

The purpose of this case study is to illustrate how policy analysis research was used to guide new policy development for a financial aid scholarship program at the University of Texas at Austin. A brief background of the circumstances surrounding the need for policy analysis research will provide a context for understanding the procedures and techniques we used. The background context will be followed by a description of how the five stages of the policy analysis research were conducted. The case study will end with an evaluation of the policy developed and highlight how the results differed from traditional policy development without the aid of policy analysis research.

Background. Prior to 1996, the University of Texas at Austin used two scholarship programs—The Texas Achievement Award (TAA) and the Texas Academic Honors Award (TAHA)—to recruit and retain underrepresented minority students. These scholarship programs were one part of a larger affirmative action plan to increase the ethnic diversity of the campus. The goals of the scholarship program were to attract bright, well-prepared African-American and Hispanic students to not only enroll but to persist through graduation. The underlying philosophy of this program was based on academic excellence. Recipients were awarded scholarships on the basis of high academic accomplishment as indicated by high school class rank, standardized admissions test scores, and a track record of challenging courses in a college preparatory high school curriculum. Indicators of student leadership in various extracurricular activities were part of the selection criteria as well. The scholarship program provided annual, renewable funds to each student who met a specific academic performance criterion of a 2.25 cumulative grade point average. The scholarship amounts varied from $1,000 to $5,000 per year for up to five years of assistance. Each year more than $1 million dollars were distributed to students through this program.

On March 18, 1996, the Fifth Circuit Court rendered the Hopwood decision and a subsequent ruling by the Texas Attorney General's Office prohibited public colleges and universities from using a student's racial or ethnic background as a consideration in any recruitment, admission, or retention activities. Consequently, the scholarship programs were dismantled. The university was faced with developing a new scholarship policy within the constraints of the Hopwood decision that would embrace the university's commitment to a diverse campus (The Texas Strategic Plan, 1995–1996). When racial background could not be used as one of the selection criteria, how could the policy driving the award program be changed yet stay within the letter and intent of the law? What new standards could be set? How would recipients be selected?

Good policy development necessarily must begin with a statement of philosophy and values. The financial aid director crafted a statement of philosophy used to generate the underlying policy (Burt, 1996). This statement of philosophy shifted the scholarship program from one based on academic merit and ethnic background to one based on financial need with academic merit evaluated on the basis of the student's ability to overcome adverse socioeconomic conditions and his or her ability to perform at high levels relative to peers with the same circumstances. Clearly, this change in philosophy would dictate new policy. This written statement of philosophy not only became the foundation for the development of new policy, but it also guided the policy analysis research process from beginning to end. Because the ensuing policy analysis research methodology depended so strongly on this statement of philosophy and values, a brief presentation of the key components follows.

Values Guide Policy Development and Research Analysis. Traditionally, college and university financial aid award scholarship programs have been based on meritocracy. Only students who performed at high levels of academic performance, typically defined in absolute terms using an admission test score, a "required" high school grade point average, or a minimum standing within one's high school graduating class are considered for the scholarship funds. One outcome of this financial award philosophy was that students who attended the best preparatory high schools were more likely to earn the scholarships. Historically, these students were middle class and attended good suburban high schools with a rich college preparatory curriculum. Prior to 1996, most of the TAA and TAHA scholarship dollars were awarded to middle-class minority students. Students from disadvantaged socioeconomic backgrounds were less likely to earn these scholarships.

The goal of the new Presidential Achievement Scholarship (PAS) program was to identify students from socioeconomically disadvantaged backgrounds who may have attended an academically inferior high school but found a way to excel academically at much higher levels than their peers within the very same high school and socioeconomic circumstances. The commitment to and valuing of diversity remained a high priority for the university, but the policy guiding the selection criteria had to be rewritten. To achieve diversity, a new population of students had to be identified. The university chose to place a high value on helping students who had not considered a major research university as a possible college choice. Absolute academic meritocracy was redefined in terms of academic excellence in the face of adverse socioeconomic circumstances. At this point, the director of financial services approached the author and requested assistance in conducting the basic policy analysis research to develop, simulate, test, and evaluate the policies for this new scholarship program—one that emphasized a student's ability to overcoming adversity and achieve.

Clarify the Policy Research Analysis Expectations. Policy analysis research begins with the researcher meeting the individual or committee responsible for the policy development to define and clarify what the policy analysis research outcomes will be. In this project, the author and the director discussed how to set the policy standards for selecting student scholarship recipients. What data indicators would summarize a student's socioeconomic background? Who is "economically disadvantaged"? How would we recognize such a student? What distinguishes an academically excellent high school from an inferior one? What indicators define excellence relative to one's peers in similar circumstances? These discussions are necessary at the very beginning, but they continue throughout the many iterations of policy simulation and evaluation. Numerous suggestions were discussed, debated, and discarded but eventually we agreed on the categories of information that would define the policy standards for selecting scholarship recipients. We agreed to define the award policy according to where students ranked on an "adversity index" that represented a numerical summary of a student's socioeconomic background, the quality of the high school attended, and an indication of how well prepared each student was for college relative to his or her peers in the same high school. This adversity index would be combined with a more traditional measure of academic performance to identify three possible financial award levels: high honors, honors, and admitted. The final research analysis product would consist of a set of computer algorithms and summary statistics that would define the policy enabling the director to select the student recipients at each scholarship award level. The grid below shows the relationship of the adversity index and academic performance to the scholarship awards.

		Adversity Index		
Academic rank	None	Moderate	Substantial	Extreme
High honors	Award	Award	Award	Award
Honors	No award	No award	Award	Award
Admitted	No award	No award	Award	Award

Without these agreements, the policy analysis research could not begin. With them, the next step required the identification of information and database elements to operationalize the adversity and academic indexes.

Identifying Data for the Index. The student affairs policy analyst must translate the policymakers' goals, values, and vision into a concrete set of policy guidelines that aid the implementation and eventual evaluation of the policy. That means taking abstract concepts and building practical data definitions that summarize the concepts. Then, data sources must be identified to build computer databases for the policy analysis and simulation stages. In this project, the author worked closely with the director of financial services to identify possible sources of data for building a numerical indicator that would operationalize the adversity index. Indicators of the student's socioeconomic status are collected as part of the College Board and the American College Testing Program's standardized admissions assessment programs. A data tape with several socioeconomic indicators for all admitted students from the previous year was obtained. Information about the student's high school was available in a statewide database provided by the Texas Education Agency (TEA). This database provided "quality" indicators for each public high school in the state of Texas in the Academic Excellence Information System (AEIS) via an internet web page (TEA, 1998). Information about the students' standardized admission test scores and high school rank were available from the admissions application and were stored in the campus student information system. For this project, the primary problem was not finding the data sources, but reducing the volume of data to simple, summary indicators. For example, the high school statewide database had hundreds of data elements on each school, including the number of students who passed state-mandated achievement tests, the amount of money spent per pupil, the number of students qualifying for the federal lunch program, and the percentage of students who took and achieved an SAT test score above 1000.

Once the data sources were identified, the complex task of bringing these disparate data elements together into a working database was initiated. Decisions were made about which of the many data elements would best define the overall concepts of high academic achievement and adversity. In building these databases, a balance between adequate representation of the underlying concept and the need for a few simple, understandable data elements was needed. In the end, for the adversity index we identified three socioeconomic indicators, five indicators of school quality, and one indicator of peer performance. We also used high school class rank from the admissions database as an indicator of high academic achievement. The three socioeconomic indicators also were taken from new data elements on the admission application form. They consisted of mother's educational level, father's educational level, and estimated family income. All five of the indicators of school quality were taken from the TEA database. The first four items consisted of the percentage of students in the high school who (1) qualified for the federal lunch program, (2) passed the statewide achievement TAAS exams, (3) took the SAT or ACT college admissions tests, and (4) achieved an SAT score of 1120 or an ACT score of 26. The fifth item was the average SAT/ACT score for the high school. The peer performance indicator was also taken from the TEA database and it was represented by the following calculation: student's SAT/ACT score divided by the average SAT/ACT score of the student's high school divided by the percentage of the students in the high school taking the SAT/ACT.

To arrive at these indicators, many other possible indicators were tried and discarded during the policy simulation stage. In addition, repeated discussions were held with university decision makers in an open debate at many points during the development stage to ensure that the final set of indicators reflected the values (stage 1) of the university. One consequence of this method of policy research analysis is that more data must be included in the construction of the database than may be needed. Unlike traditional educational research, where only a predefined set of data elements are included for analysis, policy analysis research requires a greater breadth in quality and kind of data elements. Because the purpose of policy analysis research is to identify the best combination of factors to shape a given policy, the researcher must conduct exploratory data analysis, and it is easier to put a wide variety of data into a database at the beginning than it is to reconstruct a database at a later time.

One of the problems with building a policy analysis database is that the disparate data elements must be linked by individual student record. Hence, information from the admissions database had to cross-link to the statewide high school database. For this project, the data indicators from the TEA high school database were identified by a high school code and linked to a different high school code used during the admissions testing phase. A cross-link database was constructed to bring the two sets of data into a common database for the next stage of the policy research, the analysis of data.

Selecting Data Analysis Techniques. In the third stage of this policy analysis research project, we selected the appropriate statistical analyses for building and analyzing the academic merit and adversity indicators. The selection of an appropriate data analysis technique is a function of many factors, but one of the most important is the form of the data that make up the policy database. The form of the data elements limits the statistical analysis, and policy analysis research routinely demands data in many different forms, much of which are categorical or qualitative in nature. Consequently, many of the traditional statistical methods may not be used.

For this project, we used the exploratory data analytic tools suggested by Tukey (1977). For each of the data elements, we generated simple frequency distributions to understand the range and shape of the data. The goals of the program were to identify no more than 5 percent of the student applicants for possible financial scholarship awards, yet within that small group very discriminating decisions had to be made. Hence, the adversity index had to be constructed in such a way to set a cutting score at a high level, yet provide a way to spread students across three scholarship categories. In technical terms, the adversity index award indicator had to have a highly skewed data distribution in the positive direction. To achieve the desired shape and form for this index, we looked at each data element and assigned points such that the top 5 percent of the data distribution would receive a large number of points, the next 10 percent would receive fewer points, the next 10 to 15 percent only a small number of points, and the bottom 70 to 75 percent of any given data distribution would receive no points. For example, the distribution of the percentage of students participating in the federal lunch program within the Texas high schools was generated and the following points assigned as shown in the grid below.

Percentage of students in high school federal lunch program	Assigned points	Percentage in category
Less than 42	0	70.0
42–52	2	15.8
53–67	3	10.6
Greater than 67	5	6.6

This kind of point assignment was made for each data element and the points were summed to provide an overall adversity index that ranged in value from 0 to 69. That distribution was then used to determine three award levels. These three award levels, called extreme adversity, substantial adversity, and moderate adversity, were cross-tabulated with the academic merit indicator of high school rank. Hence, students who were in the top 5 percent of their graduating class and in the top 5 percent of the adversity index would receive a $5,000 renewable scholarship for four years. Students in other combinations of adversity or high school class rank would receive differing amounts of scholarship money.

The assignment of points to the adversity indicator based on the percentages of students that fell at certain points was an important part of the next stage, called policy analysis simulation. It was through repeated iterations of assigning points, reexamining the data distributions, and adjusting the number of points assigned that a balance between the subcomponents of the family socioeconomic, the school, and the peer performance indicators was achieved. This is a particular strength of policy analysis research and will be described in some detail in the next section.

Simulating Policy Decisions. The fourth stage in conducting policy analysis research is to conduct policy simulations by creating the conditions under which the new policy might be applied, examining the results, adjusting the policy to further refine the possible outcomes, and then reapplying the "new" policy and reexamining the outcomes again. The number of simulations is unpredictable and depends on how well the policy produces the expected results. For the financial scholarship program, points were assigned to the data elements and new cutting points established numerous times. By applying the points to an entire population of admitted students, the number of awards and the amount of money could be related to the pool of potential recipients. In addition, part of the simulation provided for the opportunity to generate statistical profiles of these potential recipients. The statistical profiles were based on the data elements comprising the selection criteria for the scholarships. Hence, at the end of each policy simulation, the potential pool of award recipients could be compared with those who had not qualified under that simulation analysis. These statistical profiles allowed the decision maker and research policy analyst an opportunity to fine-tune the outcomes, not only in the number of students who received awards, but also in terms of the selection criteria defining the adversity index. If the selection criteria selected too many students for a given category of scholarship recipient, the cutting points for the award selections could be adjusted. Likewise, if the policy simulation analysis provided awards to the "wrong" students, the number of points could be reassigned to a more desirable mix.

These policy simulations form the heart of policy analysis research because the results of "applying" the policy to a particular group of students could be evaluated, adjusted, and reapplied before having to make a "final" decision about the policy standards. In the case of the financial scholarships, the number of students qualifying within a pool of admitted students could be estimated. In addition, a statistical profile of the potential award recipients allowed the decision makers an opportunity to make judgments about the "correctness" of their policy decisions. That is, were the "right" students ending up with the awards? At one point during the policy simulation analysis for this project, the results were shared with the president and executive officers of the university. Questions were raised about how points were assigned to students based on a single parent rather than a two-parent family. The statistical profile was examined and an adjustment in the points for the estimated family income was made. The "new" point system was tried for the entire admitted class to see whether a different point weighting system provided a more equitable selection of students from single-parent families. Arriving at an appropriate number of points for this category of student within the larger population required several iterations, but ultimately led to an acceptable outcome for the decision makers. Without these many simulations of the policy, the final outcome for a dramatically new and different approach to select scholarship recipients would not have been possible. The next stage, validating the policy, is important if we want to evaluate how well our new policy standards work.

Validating the Policy Outcomes. Although the policy simulations allow the policy to be applied and evaluated "before" it is implemented, all possible outcomes cannot be anticipated. Ultimately, the test of time must be applied and the "real" results gathered and evaluated. If the outcomes are successfully achieved, the policy may remain in effect without further modification. However, the more likely scenario is that unanticipated outcomes occur and additional refinements must be made in the policy. In the financial scholarship policy analysis project, more than $1,000,000 was offered to more than 700 students. Of these scholarship offers, more than 500 accepted the scholarship and enrolled. Because more weight was given to financial need and less weight given to academic merit, we could not predict how well these students would fare in the classroom. When compared to the nonscholarship holders, the recipients had lower standardized test scores but higher high school class rank. These students had a history of overcoming the adversity of a lower socioeconomic status and attended a school that may not have prepared them for college. One type of evidence used to evaluate the policy was whether these students would succeed academically and return for their sophomore year. At the time of publication, students selected for this scholarship were in the middle of their second semester of college. The long-range outcome data to evaluate and validate the policy more fully remain to be collected. However, based on the students' first semester academic grade performance, these scholarship recipients did very well. By traditional measures of academic preparation these students did not look as competitive as their peers in the classroom, but their cumulative GPA was 2.85 compared to the university-wide average of 2.75. The policy analysis research conducted to establish the scholarship award criteria identified students with a track record of handling adversity.

Conclusion

If student affairs professionals create or modify policy, they should do it well. Policy analysis research provides a tool to improve our policies. But policy analysis research is more than just a tool; it is an attitude that demands the systematic evaluation of how our policy influences the lives of students. When policymakers collaborate with student affairs research professionals in both the creation and the evaluation of policy, students will benefit.

References

Burt, L. "Scholarship Awarding Employing a Disadvantaged Index." Office memo. The University of Texas. August, 1996.

Texas Education Agency. "The 1996–97 Academic Excellence Indicator System Reports."
    Texas Education Agency, Austin, Tx. [http://www.tea.state.tx.us/perfreport/aeis/index.html].
    1998.
Tukey, J.W. *Exploratory Data Analysis.* Reading, Mass.: Addison-Wesley, 1977.

*GARY R. HANSON is coordinator of student affairs research at the University of Texas
at Austin.*

Technologies that may be used to search for, gather, analyze, and disseminate information during the research process are explored. Focal points are networked computer technologies and technologies for facilitating survey research.

Applications of Technology to Assist Student Affairs Researchers

Elizabeth A. Williams, Cary M. Anderson

Commenting on potential trends brought about by the increasing presence of technology on our campuses, Hanson (1997) predicted that "technology will expand our ability to acquire, interpret, and communicate complex information about the nature of student life and the effectiveness of our services to multiple audiences" (p. 42). The purpose of this chapter is to explore some of the technologies that may be used to search for, gather, analyze, and disseminate information during the research process. The first half of this chapter will focus on networked computer technology; the second half will focus on technologies for facilitating survey research.

Networked Computer Technology

The increase of student use of networked computers for communication has added both inquiry topics and a means by which to gather data for the student affairs researcher. This section focuses on using computer network applications such as e-mail, electronic discussion groups, and the World Wide Web in the research process. Information technologies are intrinsically dynamic phenomena and, as such, any attempt to portray the state of the art will be outdated as quickly as it was written. Nevertheless, gaining a general understanding of the concepts regarding the use of networked computing allows researchers to begin applying the technology.

Computer-Mediated Communication. Computer applications such as e-mail, electronic discussion groups, and World Wide Web browsers fall under the broader heading of computer-mediated communication (CMC), which is defined as the integration of computers and telecommunications for the transmission of signals over distances (Kellerman, 1993). With CMC, the computer acts as a *channel* for communication: The user or the Web page author—not the computer—is the *source* of information.

CMC allows the user, with the assistance of software, to save, forward, format, enhance, summarize, abbreviate, and encrypt information and correct errors. Digitalization makes the manipulation of data highly efficient (Newhagen and Rafaeli, 1996). CMC is interactive: Instead of simply receiving a message to interpret alone, the user can request immediate clarification from the sender. Interactivity makes computer communication a more democratic process as well as an ideal method for conducting survey research.

Asynchronicity permits the communication process to be more flexible and convenient because the message sender and the receiver do not have to be connected at the same time. Asynchronicity benefits researchers, who maintain a nine to five schedule, and their student population, who are most active from 5 P.M. onward. CMC is also insensitive to physical distance, providing for instantaneous communication whether connected to students across campus or on the other side of the globe. All of the aforementioned qualities of computer-mediated communication transform communication into an easier, faster, and more efficient process.

Information Gathering Using CMC. Information can be gathered via CMC during all stages of the research process. Using electronic mail discussion groups is a good way to begin. Discussion groups consist of subscribers who have a common interest in a particular subject. These lists are usually automated mailing systems that allow subscribers to send e-mail to one address, whereupon their message is automatically copied and sent directly to the e-mail account of all others who participate in the mailing list. Messages can be read only by subscribers to the list. In turn, the subscriber is able to respond to either an individual or the entire list membership. Listserv is a common software program used to implement electronic discussion groups. Discussion groups can be excellent sources for presenting ideas to colleagues or asking for assistance on a particular aspect of the research process. Lists devoted to student affairs topics usually focus on a functional area such as residence life or student activities. Other listervs are dedicated to the research process. Electronic discussion groups can be monitored to provide background information for a study or to collect qualitative data. Many discussion groups are archived, thus providing historical records of conversations. Simple instructions and helpful shortcuts for joining electronic discussion groups are found at the *Student Affairs Virtual Compass* (www.studentaffairs.com) maintained by Brown and Hedges (1998).

Another method for finding information during the research process is searching the World Wide Web. Using computer programs called search engines, researchers can explore the entire Web for information on a particular topic. There are two types of search engines, each with particular benefits and drawbacks. Closed-ended engines rely on human editors who attempt to organize Web pages into broad categories (for example, education) and narrower subcategories (e.g. colleges and universities→United States→Massachusetts and so on). Closed-ended engines are best when researching a broad, popular topic that human editors are likely to have assigned a subcategory. Closed-ended search engines can be time consuming, especially when looking for obscure or highly academic sites. *Yahoo!* (www.yahoo.com) is an example of a closed-ended search engine.

Conversely, open-ended search engines try to match inquiries to exact words in their immense databases and depend entirely on their own artificial intelligence to determine which Web pages match the requested search. Examples include *HotBot* (www.hotbot.com) and *AltaVista* (www.altavista.digital.com). Using an open-ended search engine is most effective when researching a narrow or esoteric topic. Unfortunately, open-ended searches often yield many more pages than needed and users are therefore required to sort through the results. As artificial intelligence technology improves, so will open-ended search engines; therefore, locating relevant Web resources eventually may become the easiest part of the on-line research process.

Many student affairs-related sites also have a presence on the Web. The *Student Affairs Virtual Compass* (www.studentaffairs.com) is a useful site that offers information and links to over 600 student affairs listervs and websites. Elling (1998) maintains a web page specific to student affairs and institutional research (http://www.uncc.edu/stuaffairs/salinks.htm) with links to college and university offices that specialize in student affairs research, as well as links to other related resources. In addition, Milam (1998) designed a Web page with links valuable to the institutional researcher (http://apollo.gmu.edu/~jmilam/air95.html).

The Web also can provide a researcher with connections to more traditional materials such as the *ERIC Clearinghouse on Higher Education* (http://www.gwu.edu/~eriche/) and access to many academic libraries, which in turn are connected to a plethora of valuable resources such as *OCLC First Search, PsycLit,* or digitalized journals. Start with connecting to an institutional library and follow the links to the information desired. Some libraries restrict access, but guest access may be granted through the host librarian.

Technologies for Facilitating Survey Research

Over the past two decades, a variety of technological innovations have affected the administration of telephone and self-administered surveys dramatically as well as the analysis of resulting data. Technologies such as computer-assisted telephone interviewing (CATI), optical mark reading (OMR) desktop scanners, computer-mediated communication (CMC), and PC-based software for analyzing data have increased the ease with which survey data can be collected and analyzed. As is the case with other technological innovations, the application of these increasingly sophisticated technologies requires initial investments of financial resources (to purchase necessary hardware or software) and time (to learn how to use the applications). However, substantial payoff is often achieved by incorporating these technologies into existing survey research efforts or by creating new research mechanisms. The remainder of this chapter is devoted to discussing the practical application of CATI software, OMR scanners, CMC, and PC-based data analysis software for survey researchers in student affairs.

Computer-Assisted Telephone Interviewing. Essentially, CATI technology allows interviewers to read survey questions to respondents off a computer screen and enter data directly into the computer. Questionnaires are "programmed" using a CATI software package (for example, *Ci3, Results for Research,* or *The Survey System*), and the survey can be administered by using floppy disks for each individual work station, the hard drives of individual computers, or a fileserver of a Local Area Network (LAN). Previous to the development of CATI technology approximately fifteen years ago, telephone interviewers typically read questionnaire items to respondents off a paper copy of the survey and marked responses by hand directly onto paper sheets. Subsequent to data collection, the data for each survey were entered into a computer file manually by using a data entry program such as *dbase.*

CATI offers substantial advantages to the student affairs researcher. First and foremost, since data are entered directly into a computer file by interviewers as they are interviewing respondents, the costly and time-consuming process of a separate data entry step is eliminated; once the interviewing process has been completed, the data can be analyzed almost immediately. For example, Project Pulse, the weekly telephone polling operation of the Student Affairs Research, Information, and Systems office (SARIS) at the University of Massachusetts Amherst, typically conducts interviewing on Tuesday evenings and produces preliminary results the next day, subsequent to "merging" the data from the twenty-five or so floppy disks that were used by the interviewers to administer the survey.

Second, CATI systems typically incorporate a variety of features that diminish the possibility of error on the part of interviewers. One of the most significant of these features is the ability to program "skip logic" so that it occurs automatically, without a need for decision making on the part of the interviewer. For example, surveys often include items that are designated to be answered by some respondents but not others (for example, a survey might include some questions applicable only to female respondents, not males, and vice versa). CATI questionnaires can be programmed to automatically "skip" certain questions based on a respondent's answer to a previous question. Because the programmer of the CATI questionnaire, rather than the telephone interviewer, bears the burden of correctly programming a survey's skip logic, complex skip patterns can be incorporated into surveys—patterns that would be too complicated for telephone interviewers to implement. Another CATI feature that enhances the interviewer's ability to administer the questionnaire properly is the "Help" key. Special instructions can be programmed to appear on the computer screen whenever the designated "Help" key on the computer keyboard is pressed by the interviewer. These instructions can be used to remind interviewers of any special instructions that might accompany particular survey items or provide suggestions for probes.

Another advantageous feature of CATI systems is that they can be programmed to record the duration of individual interviews, as well as the number of seconds it takes interviewers to ask each item within the survey. Prior to data analysis, these recorded times can be examined to verify the validity of each data record. For example, the recorded times can be used to identify interviewers who may be reading questions too fast, or who may be skipping transition sentences between batteries of items. Occasionally, telephone interviewers fabricate data, recording responses without actually interviewing subjects. Examining the recorded times for both complete interviews and the individual items within the questionnaire facilitates the identification of falsified data.

CATI software packages are quite versatile and can be used for research-related purposes other than telephone interviewing. For example, the *Ci3* CATI software is valuable as a data entry program because it is especially user friendly, and also contains built-in mechanisms for reducing data entry error. In addition, *Ci3* also can be used for computer-assisted personal interviewing (CAPI), whereby surveys are self-administered by respondents using personal computers either in their homes or at a central campus location.

Without question, CATI technology facilitates the conducting of telephone surveys tremendously. The multiple benefits reaped by implementing CATI are well worth the negligible price of the software (for example, basic CATI software packages can be purchased for as little as $500). In fact, given that CATI eliminates the need for separate data entry, the software typically "pays for itself" after only a few applications.

Optical Mark Reading Scanners. An OMR scanner is a machine that "reads" data from printed paper forms (commonly called *bubble sheets*) that pass under the scanner's reflected light read head. Many people are familiar with scannable forms, since they are being used increasingly for self-administered questionnaires (such as the American Council on Education/Cooperative Institutional Research Program's [ACE/CIRP] yearly survey of college freshmen), exams (such as the SAT), college and university course evaluations, and other data collection purposes. Scannable forms typically consist of multiple choice questions to which people respond by "filling in" with a pen or pencil the tiny bubble, circle, or square corresponding to their answer or response. Essentially, the scanner's read head detects either the presence or absence of a "mark" in a particular field (or bubble) by measuring the amount of infrared light that is reflected off the paper form; a bubble that is filled in reflects substantially less light than the surrounding white paper. This binary information for each field (marked/not marked) is subsequently translated into meaningful data through the use of an accompanying software program. Once forms have been read by a scanner, the resulting survey or test data can be analyzed promptly via any number of software packages.

Although OMR scanning technology has existed for approximately thirty years, it has become increasingly sophisticated and user friendly over time. A variety of desktop scanners currently are available that feature different degrees of automation and sophisticated optional features. Such features include the capabilities to read both sides of a form simultaneously, print an identifier number on each form as it passes through, and read marks made by ink as well as pencil. Original scannable surveys can be created in-house with specialized software, such as NCS's *Design Expert for Windows* or Bubble Publishing's *Form Shop* (which is more user friendly). This software automatically positions the "skunk marks" and "timing marks" (marks that assist the scanner in "reading" the form) on each scannable page, and positions the bubbles in-line with the timing marks. Once a scannable survey is created, it must be printed on white reflective paper by either a commercial or campus-based printer capable of doing high-precision printing. For the surveys to be processed by the OMR scanner, the timing marks, skunk marks, and bubbles must be aligned precisely on the page.

As is the case with CATI, the most substantial benefit of using OMR technology for survey research is the elimination of the time-consuming and expensive process of manual data entry. An automated desktop scanner (in other words, one that does not need to be fed manually) can read data from hundreds of surveys in minutes, saving many hours of labor and facilitating timely analysis of the survey data. Obviously, the benefit of using a scanner increases in magnitude with longer surveys and larger numbers of respondents.

The financial investment required to implement OMR technology is substantial compared to CATI: desktop scanners and their accompanying software typically cost between $10,000 and $20,000. Thus, whereas a CATI system may "pay for itself" over the course of one or two survey projects, a desktop scanner will not do so as quickly. Nevertheless, OMR technology is a sound investment for student affairs research offices that survey hundreds or even thousands of respondents each year by mail or in-person. As anyone who is familiar with the laborious process of manual data entry can attest, the efficiency afforded by implementing OMR technology for survey research over the long term is well worth the initial financial investment.

Computer-Mediated Communication. In theory, practically any survey of college students could be conducted with CMC technologies such as electronic mail. However, electronic mail represents a fairly new method for conducting survey research and much remains to be learned about its effectiveness. For example, Morphew and Williams (1998) found that use of an electronic mail mode to survey undergraduate students with e-mail accounts yielded a substantially lower response rate (26.5 percent) than did administering the same survey instrument by telephone. Because the reliability of survey data hinges upon obtaining an adequate response rate, potential users of CMC techniques should consider the advantages and disadvantages carefully.

Because not all students presently have access to or an aptitude for using networked computers, CMC is most appropriate for surveying special student populations. For example, CMC surveying is ideal when a survey pertains to literacy of computer users or when examining students studying abroad. However, as increasing proportions of students obtain access to computers and become proficient with CMC technologies, this technique may become more suitable for surveying on a wider array of topics.

Delivery Procedure. Unless all students within an institution use a standard electronic mail package, questionnaires should be designed to ensure optimum readability on as many different types of electronic mail systems as possible. To achieve maximum deliverability, surveys should be sent in ASCII (pronounced ask-ee) mode. ASCII mode is a simple text format that allows for translation of text characters from one type of operating system (for example, Novell, UNIX, VM) to another. To prepare an ASCII survey, use nonproportional typeface (for example, Courier), at a maximum of sixty characters per line. A hard break, instead of an automatic wrap, should be placed after each line. Although this layout method is not as visually appealing as a desktop published questionnaire, the tradeoff in terms of the increased likelihood of delivery in the proper format is worth the loss in visual appeal.

As an alternative to ASCII, the survey could be sent as an attachment (if your system allows) to be opened by the recipient in a word processing program, such as Microsoft Word or WordPerfect. Word processing software is often more user friendly than electronic mail software in terms of editing documents such as a survey. Therefore, attachments can increase the ease with which respondents complete surveys.

Once the format for creating and sending the survey is determined, the survey should be sent *directly* to the intended respondents and not through discussion list software. Because membership on discussion groups is in constant flux, it is not possible to calculate sample size accurately when sending surveys through discussion lists. To calculate a survey's response rate, sample size must be known. Therefore, the only way to be confident of sample size is to control precisely to whom the surveys are sent.

In addition to sending the survey directly to intended respondents, messages should be sent individually rather than to a group simultaneously. This technique avoids a lengthy header and increases the likelihood of confidentiality. A header is the information at the top of an electronic mail message providing the user name, client computer address, date and time of mailing, and other technical data required for accurate delivery. Sending a single electronic mail message to a large number of respondents generates a large header, resulting in disclosure of the names of the participants and therefore compromising confidentiality. In addition, the questionnaire appears several screens later in the message, which may discourage participation by potential respondents.

To ensure optimum deliverability and return of an e-mail survey, check with the computer system administrator to ensure that no maintenance or software changes/upgrades are scheduled during the project's mailing activity. Changes or upgrades to the network could seriously hamper the research project.

Response Options. Participants should be offered different options for responding to the survey. One method is the use of a World Wide Web page. Respondents can complete and submit the survey using a Web browser interface (for example, Netscape, Microsoft Explorer, Lynx). If this technique is selected, Web pages should be designed to support both graphical and text-based Web browsers. The text-based interface is particularly important, since potential respondents may have access to less sophisticated computing equipment and software and may choose to have their graphical capabilities turned off because of internet connection costs. Hanson (1997) provided an example of Web page data collection. As with all scientific surveys, sample size must be known. It would be inappropriate to post a Web page containing a survey and have people respond at random; there would be no way to determine the reliability of the data. Be sure to establish a method for respondent verification with the goal of preventing the random Web surfer from tainting data. Asking for e-mail addresses achieves this goal and has the added benefit of providing an updated mailing list.

Another method for gathering completed e-mail questionnaires is encouraging the respondent to fill out the electronic mail survey by editing the answers (in other words, by placing an asterisk by the response to multiple choice questions and typing in the answer to open-ended questions) and then returning the edited copy by using the "reply" feature of the e-mail software. For many users, this is the most convenient method to respond to electronic mail. The participant could also send a response by e-mail message indicating the original question number and corresponding answer; for example, Q1. 3 years, Q2. 3, Q3. 2, etc. Further, the use of file attachments, as discussed previously, works well for those with more sophisticated e-mail software packages.

Finally, the researcher should allow for more traditional methods of response such as fax and postal mail. As e-mail software becomes more user friendly and more features are added, challenges regarding responding to questionnaires will be greatly reduced. Yet for now, several return options should be offered.

Undeliverable Messages. One potential problem of using CMC to collect survey data is that messages sometimes "bounce" back because of invalid or unknown electronic addresses. According to Krol (1994), electronic mail usually cannot be delivered for three reasons: (1) the mail system cannot locate the recipient's host computer system; (2) the recipient is unknown at the host computer to which the message was sent; or (3) some other technical difficulty (for example, the remote system may be misconfigured or dead).

Undeliverable messages do not necessarily mean an addressee has physically moved. In many cases, the recipient's e-mail address may have been changed or updated during a system or software upgrade. When this occurs, messages may be forwarded for a period of time, similar to the forwarding of postal mail. Researchers should make sure that e-mail addresses are updated and plan for undeliverable messages.

Confidentiality. Maintaining confidentiality is a special concern for the researcher who uses CMC, because e-mail messages have headers that reveal the sender's identity. If a respondent attempts to return a completed questionnaire but for some reason it is bounced back to the respondent, that completed survey could also be forwarded to the electronic mail postmaster of the respondent's institution. Postmasters receive copies of returned messages so they can correct any technical problems with an address or system. Although this process is necessary technologically, the disadvantage is that the postmaster has access to the respondents' answers to the questionnaire, thus compromising confidentiality. Professional standards and ethics, along with the simple reality that postmasters rarely have time to read bounced messages, dictate that confidentiality is likely to be maintained; however, this issue must be acknowledged.

Using a Web page can eliminate potential confidentiality problems of e-mail surveys. However, when collecting confidential data via the Web, secure transfer methods should be used to send data, like those used to send credit card information via the internet. Although there are efficiency and geographic benefits to using CMC in the survey process, it is important that the risks of sending confidential information via CMC be disclosed.

PC-Based Software for Data Analysis. Anyone who processed and analyzed survey data prior to the advent of the personal computer can attest to the arduous and time-consuming processes entailed in accomplishing these tasks. After surveys had been completed by respondents (or data had been recorded by telephone interviewers using pencil and paper), it was necessary to keypunch the individual data records onto cards that would be "read" by a card-reading machine attached to a mainframe computer. Once a data set was compiled, it was typically stored on a reel-to-reel magnetic tape that needed to be "loaded" onto the mainframe. Each time data were analyzed, the appropriate tape would have to be loaded on the mainframe computer and cards "punched" with the appropriate instructions for the computer; the computer would then print out the results of data runs (for example, frequencies, cross-tabulations, etc.). For those who conducted data analysis in the aforementioned fashion, data analysis software packages for personal computers (for example, *SPSS, SAS, Systat*) are truly "magical." The efficiency with which PC-based data analysis can be accomplished is utterly remarkable. Analyses that previously took hours, days, or even weeks to accomplish with a mainframe computer can be accomplished in seconds or minutes with a PC.

Initially, PC-based software packages were based on their mainframe counterparts and required the creation of programs that were typed into the computer by using syntax specific to the application. For example, to create a data set, a program was written specifying variable names, the column location of each variable, the variable's "type" (numeric or character/string), and accompanying value labels. Once this program was written and processed by the PC, other programs could be run to obtain frequencies for the variables in the data set, do cross-tabulations, run ANOVAs, etc.

Within the past five years, PC-based data analysis software has been developed that is Windows-based. Both SPSS and SAS have developed Windows versions of their software that are incredibly user friendly and even more efficient than their DOS-based predecessors. With these applications, there is no need to type in command language; instead, the desired "procedures" (for example, frequencies, recoding, selecting cases, etc.) are selected with a mouse and menus. One tremendous advantage to "clicking" on commands rather than typing them in is the elimination of typographical errors such as misspelled variable names, missing periods at the end of command lines, misplaced commas, and the like. With DOS-based applications, typographical errors in programs were unavoidable and commonplace; time was frequently wasted searching for error-inducing typos. Lengthy programs typically were run several times before running "clean." Another benefit of Windows-based data analysis programs is that the actual data set can be viewed in spreadsheet format while analysis is being conducted; in other words, researchers can actually see the data they are manipulating. In addition, if data entry is necessary, data can be entered directly into Windows-based software packages; there is no need to use a separate data entry software application.

Conclusion

The technological innovations discussed in this chapter have expanded considerably the variety of techniques that researchers have available to them to search for, gather, analyze, and disseminate information. Computer mediated communication practices, such as electronic mail and listservs, can be particularly useful during the initial stages of research, allowing for timely and efficient sharing of ideas and information. The World Wide Web's powerful search engines can be harnessed to access tremendous amounts of information, including electronic journal articles, databases such as the *ERIC Clearinghouse on Higher Education,* and informational sites specific to student affairs. Survey researchers can facilitate data collection by using computer-assisted telephone interviewing, optical mark reading desktop scanners, and computer-mediated communication. PC-based data analysis software packages, particularly those that are Windows-based, are invaluable tools for entering and analyzing data. When appropriately applied, each of the technologies discussed in this chapter can enhance considerably the student affairs researcher's ability to conduct thorough, efficient, and economical research.

References

Brown, S., and Hedges, A. "Student Affairs Virtual Compass: Your Guide to Internet Resources for College Student Affairs." [http://www.StudentAffairs.com]. 1998.

Elling, T. "Student Affairs Research at UNC Charlotte: Links of Interest." [http://www.uncc.edu/stuaffairs/salinks.htm]. 1998.

Hanson, G. R. "Using Technology in Assessment and Evaluation." In C. M. Engstrom and K.W. Kruger, (eds.), *Using Technology to Promote Student Learning: Opportunities for Today and Tomorrow.* San Francisco: Jossey-Bass, 1997.

Kellerman, A. *Telecommunications and Geography.* London: Belhaven, 1993.

Krol, E. *The Whole Internet: User's Guide and Catalog* (2nd Ed.) . Sebastopol, Calif.: O'Reilly and Associates, 1994.

Milam, J. H. "Internet Resources for Institutional Research." [http://www.apollo.gmu.edu/~jmilam/air95.html]. 1998.

Morphew, C. C., and Williams, A. N. "Using Electronic Mail to Survey Undergraduates: Pitfalls and Possibilities." Paper presented at the Association for Institutional Research Forum, Minneapolis, May, 1998.

Newhagen, J. E., and Rafaeli, S. "Why Communication Researchers Should Study the Internet: A Dialogue." *Journal of Communication*, 1996, *46* (1), 4–13.

ELIZABETH A. WILLIAMS is a Ph.D. candidate in the department of sociology at the University of Massachusetts Amherst.

CARY M. ANDERSON is associate dean of students at Holy Cross College.

This chapter examines opportunities for collaboration between student affairs and faculty on developing a research agenda, and the effects of higher education graduate programs on these activities.

Collaboration Between Student Affairs and Faculty on Student-Related Research

Kevin F. Grennan, Margaret A. Jablonski

As the last decade of the twentieth century began, higher education suffered a surfeit of predictions, warnings, and labels. Institutions and their leaders were warned to adapt to changes in the labor market while adhering to the broader functions of higher education (Gordon, 1993). They also were warned to prepare for new structural reorganizations as a result of "tight state budgets, intensified competition for resources, and concern for higher education's responsiveness to societal needs—undergraduate education, teacher education, minority enrollment and achievement, etc." (Callan, 1993, p. 17). The 1980s had witnessed growing concern that the whole of a college education was less than the sum of its parts, and there was no coherence (Boyer, 1993). It became ever more clear that we needed sophisticated forms of assessment to respond responsibly to the demands for accountability that surfaced in every state. Hence, the 1990s began with concerns expressed by governors, legislators, parents, and faculty about the importance and role of undergraduate education and the continuing escalation of tuition and fees. As the decade of the 1990s ends we have a National Commission on the Cost of Higher Education issuing a report that "colleges risk an 'erosion of public trust' if their charges continue to soar" (Burd, 1998, p. 1). Presidents and chancellors, administrators and faculty, will all be engaged in processes of examination and renewal. The challenge will be to do this effectively and collaboratively.

This chapter examines possibilities for research activities within student affairs, and the effect that graduate preparation programs have on those activities. The calls for research in higher education, regardless of their origin, have been primarily reactionary and not well considered. This chapter examines the opportunities for working with faculty to develop and implement a research agenda for the student affairs division. We highlight areas of collaboration and provide examples for research to help guide policy decisions on programs and services. We examine how we are preparing our master's and doctoral students to conduct research in the field of student affairs, and make suggestions for incorporating more research opportunities in the curriculum. Finally, we make recommendations for student affairs and faculty to work together in developing and implementing a research agenda on student life issues.

Research and Student Affairs

The increased pressure from students, parents, media, legislators, and accrediting agencies to provide "education" efficiently and at low cost has affected the debate over what constitutes an educated person for the twenty-first century. Colleges and universities are redesigning their curricula to meet a range of educational goals, from producing educated citizens who can function in the global economy, to addressing learning styles by adding teamwork and experiential activities to more traditional and structured lecture formats (King, 1994). The revision of undergraduate education in particular is being done by faculty with an outlook toward assessing outcomes. Some campuses are enhancing undergraduate education through collaborative activities between academic and student affairs areas (Schroeder, 1996).

Areas for Research. Student life—the wide variety of programs and services within student affairs—is also ripe for redesign of programs and services. Over the past decade institutions have begun to systematize the collection of data on student life to guide decisions around current and projected programs. Student affairs traditionally has been the area of the academy that provides the programs and services for students outside of the classroom. When we take into consideration the wide breadth of experience and learning that student affairs affects, we see an array of opportunities for conducting research. In surveying the "handbooks of the profession," one can find the following topics that lend themselves to research: campus culture, diversity issues, student cognition and learning, theories of student development, ethical behavior, leadership, legal trends, advising, mediation, technology, and graduate preparation programs themselves (Komives and Woodard, 1996; Whitt, 1997). Each of these topical areas has the potential for several, if not a multitude, of explorations. Each of these areas is also connected to other disciplines within the academy. By partnering with faculty in other fields, student affairs faculty and professional staff will enlarge their lens of inquiry into college life and student experience.

Several educators have called for a comprehensive assessment program for student life (Upcraft and Schuh, 1996; Beeler and Hunter, 1991). Upcraft and Schuh (1996) identify seven components they consider essential in a student affairs assessment program: tracking use of programs, services, and facilities;

assessing student needs; assessing student satisfaction; assessing environments and student cultures; assessing outcomes; assessing one institution by comparing it to other institutions; and using professional standards. Similarly, the choice of research topics should be done (1) to determine who are the students and what are their needs, (2) to gain information about the strengths and weaknesses of programs, and (3) to inform the management activities that most directly affect students (Beeler and Hunter, 1991).

Research studies should be designed to advance our knowledge about student behavior, learning, and interaction in communities. Research can be used to assist in the design of programs and activities that advance the development of the individual as well as the campus community. Policy and practice in student affairs needs to be informed by relevant data even if this means changing policy or practice. Research should not be conducted to justify a program or policy, but to inform policy and practice in advance.

Leadership development and group dynamics are two areas traditionally found in student activities or student development programs. Current research using naturalistic modes of inquiry considers these areas in the context of the students engaged in the programs. It is no longer acceptable to look just for a cause-and-effect intervention to produce desired leadership outcomes. Instead, new research from physics on chaos theory, wave theory, and fractals, among other topics, now challenges us to consider the unpredictable nature of action and behavior (Wheatley, 1992). To research leadership behavior, we need to explore the world of quantum physics. A natural partnership between the physical world and the social world is emerging. Wheatley (1992) and others encourage the application of the hard sciences to the study of leadership. Student affairs students and practitioners need to understand this emerging research and theory to inform practice in student affairs programs. Partnering with the physical sciences faculty to develop leadership programs would present opportunities for integrated conceptual thinking and creative program design.

Modes of Inquiry. Expanding modes of inquiry to include both quantitative and qualitative methods allows for a variety of ways to gain understanding of the problems and questions within student life. Partnering with faculty from quantitative and qualitative research backgrounds provides a richer array of data to discuss the impact of a program or department on student life. Davis (1994) and Fried (1995) suggest using multiple measures to gather data on student outcomes and gearing research toward supporting the institution's unique mission and history.

The qualitative mode of inquiry involves understanding the subject, contextualizing the problem and data, and interpreting patterns or themes inductively (Eisner and Peshkin, 1990). Such methods lend themselves to exploration of many student life issues and programs. Again, faculty from education, history, sociology, management, and women's studies, among others, who routinely use qualitative methods in their research, are natural partners for student affairs practitioners.

Research Requirements in Higher Education Preparation Programs

In the September 1997 *NASPA Forum*, the president of the National Association of Student Personnel Administrators (NASPA), Jack R. Warner, wrote of the significance of collaboration between student affairs and academic affairs professionals: "Today's realities make this collaboration more important than ever" (Warner, 1997, p. 2). Warner went on to analyze the strengths that each side brought to such collaborative efforts: "Academic affairs brings discipline-specific knowledge, highly developed methods of inquiry, and emphasis on solid research and scholarship. Student affairs brings specific knowledge of students, their needs, aspirations, and characteristics, and an understanding of how to work with them. Student affairs professionals also bring knowledge and skill in group process and collaborative decision making (p. 2).

Although this scenario is a promising one, its chances of being fully developed would be significantly enhanced if two important factors were present: student affairs practitioners with better training in research methodology, and the existence of more student affairs research offices on our campuses. This section considers the present state of graduate preparation, both doctoral and master's level programs. We then turn to the opportunities for collaboration with faculty and suggest a variety of ways to promote and enhance these efforts.

How we prepare individuals for the field of student affairs has long been a concern to the profession (Keim, 1991). Keim's (1991) longitudinal study of student affairs preparation programs found that requirements for research courses have varied only slightly at all levels of preparation. Students in doctoral programs saw the average number of required research courses drop from 3.9 in the earliest survey, which was conducted in 1973, to 3.7 in a 1987 survey. At the same time, the required number of research courses in master's level programs increased, albeit slightly, from 1.3 in 1973 to 1.4 in 1987.

Townsend's (1990) analysis of doctoral study in higher education reviewed work by Dressel and Mayhew (1974) and Crosson and Nelson (1986) that provided information about the curricula of higher education doctoral programs in the 1970s and 1980s. It is conventionally assumed that "possession of the Ph.D. indicates that its recipient is able to conduct research . . . [and] the E.D. connotes a more practitioner approach to graduate study" (Townsend, 1990, p. 171); however, this may not be a valid assumption. Neither Crosson and Nelson nor Dressel and Mayhew found significant difference between the two degrees (Townsend, 1990). Crosson and Nelson (1986) attempted to update the Dressel and Mayhew work and found there was little difference between Ph.D. and Ed.D. programs in terms of minimum total credit hours required, residency requirements, and core course requirements, but that Ph.D. programs required more research and statistics credits.

Yet details on this difference are lacking. The profile provided by Crosson and Nelson shows that forty-seven of the Ph.D. programs (89 percent) had a mandated requirement for research and statistics; however, forty-four of the Ed.D. programs surveyed (80 percent) had this mandated requirement as well.

Dill and Morrison (1985) help to fill in some of the gaps. They point out that earlier studies of distinctions between the Ed.D. and Ph.D. (Moore, Russel, and Ferguson, 1960; Robertson and Sistler, 1971) had "concluded that the distinctions between the two degrees were shadowy at best" (p. 169). In 1978, Dill and Morrison examined sixty-six doctoral programs of the eighty-one graduate programs listed in the 1977–1978 *Higher Education Directory* published by the ERIC Clearinghouse on Higher Education. Thirty-five programs offered both the Ph.D. and Ed.D., twelve offered only the Ph.D., and nineteen only the Ed.D. There were at least two and sometimes three research objectives for these programs: (1) to develop students' ability to do original, "pure," or "theoretical" research; (2) to develop the skills necessary to do a dissertation; (3) to develop the ability to read and interpret research.

The twelve Ph.D.-only and twenty-one Ph.D.-option programs stressed the first research objective; the nineteen Ed.D.-only and twenty-one Ed.D.-option programs had equal emphasis across all three areas or tended to the "applied" and "literacy" objectives. The majority of the Ed.D. programs required fewer than twelve hours of statistics or methods courses; the majority of the Ph.D. programs required twelve or more hours of such courses. However, there were sixteen programs that made no distinctions in the research requirements for the Ed.D. and Ph.D. (Dill and Morrison, 1985).

The focus on the content of the degree begs the question of the focus of the students who are engaged in the degree's work. Since a large number, if not the majority, of students in doctoral programs are already employed in higher education in administrative positions, it is unlikely that they will be more concerned with "pure" research objectives than with achieving literacy and the ability to perform applied research to satisfy the dissertation requirement. As Dill and Morrison remind us, "while 95 percent of the graduates may have perceived the Ph.D. to be a necessary credential, only a small fraction of these degree holders are actually teaching or doing research in the field of higher education" (1985, p. 177).

At the entry level of the preparation continuum, the Council for the Advancement of Standards (CAS) provides fairly detailed standards and guidelines for graduate level (M.Ed.) preparation programs. In the latest version of professional standards for higher education, CAS stipulates that "an essential feature of the preparation program must be the spirit and practice of inquiry and the production and use of research, evaluation, and assessment information by faculty and students alike" (1994, p. 174). CAS goes on to state that "studies of research methodologies and critiques of published studies are essential" (p. 175). In spite of these exhortations, Keim (1991) questioned the amount of research required in preparation programs.

The dilemma is that student affairs professionals have a wide range of duties and responsibilities, and not all want or need to have research competencies (Komives, 1992; Hunter, 1992; Townsend and Wiese, 1992; Gordon,

Strode, and Mann, 1993; Sandeen, 1988). Furthermore, it is difficult to place a high value on research and evaluation if chief student affairs officers, who hire and promote, consider those competencies "least important" (Gordon, Strode, and Mann, 1993, p. 295).

Notwithstanding, should not all student affairs professionals have a greater understanding of and appreciation for research? A hallmark of being a "professional" is having a critical understanding of the theory as well as the practice of the profession. Malaney (1993) has declared: "Student affairs researchers have been writing for decades about the importance of research within the profession. . . . During this time, NASPA has shown strong support by sponsoring research activities, encouraging the presentation of research at its national and regional conferences, and publishing research studies in the *NASPA Journal.* Most recently, NASPA published a monograph devoted entirely to student affairs research in order to spark interest throughout the profession" (Beeler and Hunter, 1991) (p. 182).

It is clear to some (Young, 1993) that if student affairs is to continue its evolution as a profession, those who would consider themselves professionals will need to have more formal training in research methodology as well as the opportunity to apply that training. It is to the application that we now turn. One way to achieve this is to develop linkages with academic departments on campus and to engage in collaborative research design, implementation, and evaluation.

Recommendations for Working More Closely with Faculty

One immediate form of linkage is between graduate preparation programs and their campuses. This would provide employment opportunities in the form of assistantships for graduate students, research projects for preparation program faculty, and examples of bridging and collaboration for all concerned. But most campuses lack access to such programs. In the majority of situations, such collaboration must and should take place with departments that have no inherent interest in higher education or student affairs research. That is the challenge.

This would mean that student affairs professionals would have to overcome some powerful biases (Creeden, 1989). Yet it would serve the needs of faculty, who have the expertise and the reward system to justify the research, as well as answer those critics of higher education who are demanding more accountability. In the end, it would also serve the student. The following recommendations are suggested for student affairs practitioners to create partnerships with faculty that will enhance the research component of student life, as well as the out-of-classroom experience for students in general.

Identify key topics for research in student affairs by involving students and faculty in the process. Identify key faculty on campus who have expertise in that area. Begin by starting small, conducting research that requires low cost and low levels of expertise (Weitzer and Malaney, 1991).

Start a research discussion group, asking faculty to participate by discussing their research with student affairs staff, providing readings for background material, etc. Highlight faculty members research in student affairs training programs, newsletters, parents' days, alumni events, etc.

Establish a faculty grant program. Award small grants of $1000 to $5000 to assist in student affairs research projects. Encourage collaboration by providing access to data for faculty to publish and present, in collaboration with student affairs staff.

Consider research questions and conduct assessment for each committee, task force, and department within student affairs. Then seek faculty with overlapping research agendas to sit on or advise the committee or department.

Provide research assistantships (RAs) for research programs/offices by offering to share some of the RA time with a faculty member who is assisting student affairs in some way. Many academic departments could use graduate student support for research projects.

Offer research courses (both quantitative and qualitative) on problems from student affairs to explore. Develop partnerships with the schools of education and management to design studies in their research courses that examine key student life problems. Consider how to structure access to data, how to interpret findings that student affairs does not agree with, and what happens to the results in publication.

Secure the support of the president or chief academic officer/provost for counting faculty time spent working with student affairs toward one course per year or one committee assignment for service to the university.

Consider appointing a Scholar in Residence to conduct research on student affairs issues. Release time should be provided for the faculty member to conduct research, conduct workshops, lead discussion groups, etc.

Design a research course for student affairs practitioners in which they would learn about research techniques and conduct research as part of their regular position on campus. The faculty leader should be given course-load credit for teaching this course. Have a forum for showcasing the research each year and publicize this in campus publications and other media.

Develop proposals with faculty for internal research grants or external grants from foundations, corporations, and governmental agencies. For example, Tinto (1998) has suggested reorganizing the academy to promote students' active involvement with others in learning. Setting up a pilot "learning community" would be a natural model for collaboration. Provide for released time and TA support for faculty members as part of the grant.

Typically, faculty members do not have access to support staff for administrative assistance such as typing, editing, and arranging meetings that student life departments have. They also do not have access to resources for supplies and meeting expenses. Student affairs offices could provide a project budget that allows faculty to be reimbursed for some expenses related to their research projects.

Conclusion

Professionals in student affairs need more understanding of the skills necessary for conceptualizing and conducting research as well as the types of research questions that would be valuable in improving programs and services. Programs for higher education preparation need to consider the structure and content of their research requirements. There is a need to build in more opportunities for research across the curriculum and for connecting theory and practice. Real problems and issues could form a greater share of the content of research courses, thus enabling students to acquire valuable, practical, and relevant experience. Looking across the disciplines enables student affairs to connect with an array of academic fields and a variety of modes of inquiry to conduct research. Student affairs research offices are the natural mechanisms for facilitating the research itself and for assisting in the development of skills for student affairs practitioners.

References

Beeler, K. J., and Hunter, D. E. *Puzzles and Pieces in Wonderland: The Promise and Practice of Student Affairs Research.* Washington, D.C.: National Association of Student Personnel Administrators, 1991.

Boyer, E. L. "Campus Climate in the 1980s and 1990s: Decades of Apathy and Renewal." In A. Levine (ed.), *Higher Education in America, 1980– 2000.* Baltimore: Johns Hopkins University Press, 1993.

Burd, S. "U.S. Panel Warns Colleges to Cut Costs or Risk an 'Erosion of Public Trust.'" *The Chronicle of Higher Education: Academe Today,* January 30, 1998 [On-line]. Available: http://chronicle.com/.

Callan, P. M. "Government and Higher Education." In A. Levine (ed.), *Higher Education in America, 1980– 2000.* Baltimore: The Johns Hopkins University Press, 1993.

Council for the Advancement of Standards in Higher Education. "Preparation Standards and Guidelines at the Master's Degree Level for Student Affairs Professionals in Higher Education" (1994). In M. C. Keim and J. W. Graham (eds.), *Directory of Graduate Preparation Programs in College Student Personnel.* Washington, D.C.: American College Personnel Association, 1994.

Creeden, J. E. "Student Affairs Biases as a Barrier to Collaboration: A Point of View." *NASPA Journal,* 1989, *26* (1), 60–63.

Crosson, P. H., and Nelson, G. M. "A Profile of Higher Education Doctoral Programs." *The Review of Higher Education,* 1986, *9* (3), 335–357.

Davis, B. G. "Demystifying Assessment: Learning from the Field of Evaluation." In J. S. Stark and A. Thomas (eds.), *Assessment and Program Evaluation.* ASHE Reader Series. Needham Heights, Mass.: Simon and Schuster, 1994.

Dill, D. D., and Morrison, J. L. "Ed.D. and Ph.D. Research Training in the Field of Higher Education: A Survey and a Proposal." *The Review of Higher Education,* 1985, *8* (2), 169–186.

Dressel, P. L., and Mayhew, L. B. *Higher Education as a Field of Study.* San Francisco: Jossey-Bass, 1974.

Eisner, E., and Peshkin, A. (eds.). *Qualitative Inquiry in Education: The Continuing Debate.* New York: Teachers College Press, 1990.

Fried, J., and Associates. *Shifting Paradigms in Student Affairs.* Lantham, Maryland: University Press of America, 1995.

Gordon, M. "The Economy and Higher Education." In A. Levine (ed.), *Higher Education in America, 1980–2000.* Baltimore: The Johns Hopkins University Press, 1993.

Gordon, S. E., Strode, C. B., and Mann, B. A. "The Mid-Manager in Student Affairs: What are CSAOs Looking For?" *NASPA Journal,* 1993, *30* (4), 290–297.

Hunter, D. E. "How Student Affairs Professionals Choose Their Careers." *NASPA Journal,* 1992, *29* (3), 181–188.

Keim, M. C. "Student Personnel Preparation Programs: A Longitudinal Study." *NASPA Journal,* 1991, *28* (3), 231–242.

King, P. M. "Theories of College Student Development: Sequences and Consequences." *Journal of College Student Development,* 1994, *35,* 413–421.

Komives, S. R. "The Middles: Observations on Professional Competence and Autonomy." *NASPA Journal,* 1992, *29* (2), 83–90.

Komives, S. R., and Woodard, D. *Student Services: A Handbook for the Profession.* 3rd ed. San Francisco: Jossey-Bass, 1996.

Malaney, G. D. "A Comprehensive Student Affairs Research Office." *NASPA Journal* (1993), *30* (3), 182–189.

Moore, H. E., Russel, J. H., and Ferguson, D. G. *The Doctorate in Education* (Vol. 2). Washington, D.C.: The American Association of Colleges for Teacher Education, 1960.

Robertson, N., and Sistler, J. K. *The Doctorate in Education: An Inquiry into Conditions Affecting Pursuit of the Doctoral Degree in the Fields of Education—The Institutions.* Bloomington, Ind.: Phi Delta Kappa, 1971.

Sandeen, A. "Careers in Student Affairs: An Introduction." In A. F. Kirby and D. Woodard (eds.), *Career Perspectives in Student Affairs.* Washington, D.C.: National Association of Student Personnel Administrators, 1988.

Schroeder, C. "Enhancing Undergraduate Education: An Imperative for Student Affairs." *About Campus,* 1996, *1* (4), 2–3.

Tinto, V. "Colleges as Communities: Taking Research on Student Persistence Seriously." *The Review of Higher Education,* 1998, *21* (2), 167–177.

Townsend, B. K. "Doctoral Study in the Field of Higher Education." In J. C. Smart (ed.), *Higher Education: Handbook of Theory and Research* (Vol. VI). New York: Agathon Press, 1990.

Townsend, B. K., and Wiese, M. "The Value of a Doctorate in Higher Education for Student Affairs Administrators." *NASPA Journal,* 1992, *30* (1), 51–58.

Upcraft, M. L., and Schuh, J. *Assessment in Student Affairs: A Guide for Practitioners.* San Francisco: Jossey-Bass, 1996.

Warner, J. R. "President's Message." *NASPA Forum,* 1997, *19* (1), 2–3.

Weitzer, W. H., and Malaney, G. D. "Of Puzzles and Pieces: Organizing and Directing a Campus-Based Research Agenda. In K. J. Beeler and D. E. Hunter (eds.), *Puzzles and Pieces in Wonderland: The Promise and Practice of Student Affairs Research.* Washington, D.C.: National Association of Student Personnel Administrators, 1991.

Wheatley, M. J. *Leadership and the New Science.* San Francisco: Berrett-Koehler Publishers, 1992.

Whitt, E. D. (ed.). *College Student Affairs Administration.* ASHE Reader Series. Needham Heights, Massachusetts: Simon and Schuster, 1997.

Young, R. B. "Examining the History of Student Affairs through the Lens of Professional Education." *NASPA Journal,* 1993, *30* (4), 243–251.

KEVIN F. GRENNAN is coordinator of the higher education program at the University of Massachusetts Amherst.

MARGARET A. JABLONSKI is visiting assistant professor at the University of Massachusetts Amherst and recent Region I vice president of the National Association of Student Personnel Administrators (NASPA).

*The student affairs research office can and should help student affairs
and the institution as a whole become a learning organization.*

Student Affairs Researcher:
Information Broker

Thomas D. Hadley

> From a very early age, we are taught to break apart problems, to
> fragment the world. This apparently makes complex tasks and sub-
> jects more manageable, but we pay a hidden, enormous price. We
> can no longer see the consequences of our actions; we lose our
> intrinsic sense of connection to the whole.
>
> Peter M. Senge (1990, p. 3)

Increasingly, student affairs organizations are responsible for the delivery of
programs and services in a highly complex and multifaceted learning environment. The array of offices and units that have evolved to serve special needs
and populations and the demand for better management tools to administer
enrollments, auxiliary functions, and student information systems reflect this
rapid transformation of student affairs work in the modern college or university. The emerging expectation that student affairs should promote learning as
articulated in *The Student Learning Imperative: Implications for Student Affairs*
requires all parts of the student affairs organization to become more purposeful in all aspects of assessment and research (American College Personnel Association, 1996).

As the array of responsibilities and call for greater emphasis on learning
within student affairs have grown, so have the needs to conduct research activities to provide guidance and direction in managing units, understanding the
needs of students, and assessing the effectiveness of our programs. The development of a student affairs research function, well documented in this monograph, has taken on many shapes and forms. Clearly, student affairs research

functions are here and will remain essential for the advancement of the student affairs agenda now and into the future.

In the recent introduction to the *Council for the Advancement of Standards (CAS) for Outcomes Assessment and Program Evaluation,* it was suggested that assessment units should employ both qualitative and quantitative methods and include the following elements (Miller, 1997):

- tracking of student use of services, programs, and facilities
- assessing student needs and wants
- assessing environments and their influences on behavior
- assessing student cultures and their influences on behavior
- assessing individual and collective outcomes of programs and services
- assessing the developmental impact of individual programs and the total collegiate experience

These are very worthy goals for any student affairs research office or function. Unfortunately, most student affairs research functions have been established for many reasons. Research units have been implemented in response to the interests of a key administrator, pressure points and demands within the various student affairs departments, or from external mandates for greater accountability. They are not often prepared to provide the comprehensive or systemic view required by *The Student Learning Imperative* or to meet the expectations of the CAS Standards.

There often is a real gap between the lofty goals and aspirations of most student affairs research functions and the reality of what most research departments really do. All too often they become a version of an institutional research function, a consulting service to help design surveys or questionnaires and collect information, or an office prepared to provide data or complete reports.

Why is there such a disparity between the possibilities of the research office and what it normally is able to do? The potential of most student affairs research functions remains unrealized because most units act and behave as though they are like any other unit within the student affairs organizational family. They do not have the tools or capacity to really transform how most student affairs organizations behave.

The Learning Organization

Peter Senge (1990), in his recent book *The Fifth Discipline: The Art and Practice of the Learning Organization,* offers some insights into why most research offices are not fully able to meet professional or institutional expectations. Senge believes that most organizations are not truly acting as learning organizations. Most members of a complex organization see themselves as having very little influence on the overall direction of that organization. They see forces beyond their professional range of responsibilities that really control events and activities of that organization. All too often the same individuals will blame outside forces for the problems within the organization. They fixate on particular events or anecdotes to understand the difficulties within the organization or try to generalize their own unique experience to define the whole experience of the organization.

The research office, like any other unit within a student affairs organization, exhibits the same learning disabilities found in any unit within a complicated organization. Although the research office is charged to help the student affairs organization expand its understanding of students, their behavior, and the learning environment, it is constrained by the same self-limiting thinking articulated by Senge.

Senge asserts that five key components will help organizations become learning organizations. Those components are as follows:

1. *Systems thinking*—All organizations and human activities are interrelated. It is a conceptual framework to focus on the whole instead of only the fragments.
2. *Personal mastery*—This is a disciplined effort of continually clarifying and deepening our understanding of our reality. We must invest the time and energy to encourage individual and organizational learning.
3. *Mental models*—Our personal mental models of reality and our work environment strongly influence our behavior. We must work to create new mental models that afford a deeper, richer view of the organization.
4. *Building shared vision*—This entails building a commitment to a collective understanding of the organization, its values, goals, and mission.
5. *Team learning*—Individuals alone are not as productive as the group. Increasing constructive and challenging discourse among members of the group increases a deeper learning that is unattainable by individuals alone.

Only when members of an organization commit themselves to these five components does Senge believe the organization is a *Learning Organization*. "Real learning gets to the heart of what it means to be human. Through learning we recreate ourselves. Through learning we become able to do something we were never able to do before. . . . Through learning we extend our capacity to create, to be part of the generative process of life" (Senge, 1990, p. 14).

Reconceptualizing Student Affairs Research

How does a student affairs researcher become an agent within the student affairs organization and the institution to foster this kind of transformative learning? Which of the five components are affected most by the work of the student affairs researcher? And finally, what are some of the implications for how the student affairs researcher views his or her role?

To help create a student affairs organization committed to Senge's view of learning, researchers should avoid the traps of defining themselves as researchers in the narrowest sense. One must begin to reconceptualize the role. A better definition may be *information broker.* Information brokers conduct research activities but perceive this as only one small component of their work. They invest a significant portion of their time in integrating all the seemingly disparate findings from assessment activities and other data from institutional sources into richer, meaningful analysis.

Most researchers tend to assume a reductionist's perspective, that is, to examine only pieces of the mosaic of the student experience. Discrete studies are conducted by looking at particular sets of issues. The findings from those studies provide data but often cannot be used really to alter prevailing belief systems or practices.

The research process should begin looking for new patterns or templates to understand the totality of student experience or the learning environment. In Senge's (1990) view, the researcher should strive to examine the trees and the forest simultaneously. Only by connecting the various pieces of the mosaic together does a broader, richer pattern emerge. The role of the student affairs researcher should be to weave a compelling story together from all the various sources of available data.

Many institutions have implemented programs to help students build their academic skills through various tutoring, supplemental instruction, or collaborative learning initiatives. Most of these activities at varying levels have been evaluated to determine whether they have an impact on student academic performance. Often the discrete measures used to determine whether programs are successful are the actual grades students receive in a particular course after taking part in the skill building intervention. Although this is an important finding, by itself it does not tell a very complete picture of the student's participation in the intervention.

To help see the forests and trees, one should examine other key variables to develop a richer understanding of the student experience. First, did students regularly attend the academic tutoring program? Often students sign up for various programs but many do not attend frequently. How can one draw conclusions about the success or failure of the intervention without examining patterns of attendance?

What kinds of students took part in the intervention? In many instances, the students who take part in the program are often B students who want to become A students. The students who have real academic deficiencies may not be the ones taking advantage of the program.

Who is teaching the course for which the intervention has been established? Faculty willing to encourage students to take part in the support program are often the ones who are caring, effective teachers in the first place. It may not be the intervention that improves student performance. It may be the commitment and support of the faculty member that has the most positive influence on student learning.

This is one example of why the student affairs researcher must be aware of the *forests* as he or she is examining the *trees*. The real learning that comes from such an analysis is not whether so many students have received better grades. The more important questions to ask are, What motivates good students to take part and why do less able students not take part? Or why do some faculty members encourage students to take advantage of support services and others do not? These kind of questions help raise more thought-provoking concerns about the learning environment and student motivation. Such inquiries encourage organizational learning that is transformative and reshapes our collective thinking about the reality of the student and institution.

Systems Thinking

Of Senge's five components, two are key elements that may be most affected by the work of the student affairs researcher: systems thinking and mental models. It is challenging to nurture a systems thinking approach to problem solving in a student affairs organization or any unit within a complicated institution such as a college or university. "We must look beyond individual mistakes or bad luck to understand important problems. We must look beyond personalities and events. We must look into the underlying structures that shape individual actions and create conditions where types of events become likely" (Senge, 1990, p. 43).

Systems thinking infers that there are intrinsic patterns and structures within the organization that have a profound effect on individual behavior (Senge, 1990). Regardless of how varied the student profile is demographically, academically, or socioeconomically, there are underlying frameworks within the institution that force most of us to see and behave in similar patterns.

For example, we often label some colleges as residential or commuter campuses given the numbers of students who either do or do not live on campus. If a campus is labeled as a commuter campus, what systems are in place at that institution that reinforce students, faculty, and administrators to behave in a particular manner? Many administrators assume commuter students will not participate in most programs and activities on campus, so fewer events and programs are offered. Some faculty may not create team-oriented projects for class assignments because they believe most commuter students will not be able to meet with other students outside of class, so these faculty rely on more traditional lecture-oriented modes of instruction. And finally, some students who may want to be active on campus might not because they perceive it to be a commuter institution!

Such a pattern of behavior is influenced strongly by an underlying systems thinking. Everyone acts as though the college is a commuter campus. All stakeholders, administrators, faculty, and students justify the lack of a vital campus life because the institution is a commuter campus!

We are not aware of how the commuter "system" inhibits ways of envisioning a different kind of institution. It is not the commuter student that alters our behavior, it is the system in which we operate that shapes our perceptions and limits our ability to see different possibilities.

Mental Models

In this instance, what can the student affairs researcher do to shift the focus from blaming commuters for an inactive campus life to examining the system that shapes our beliefs and behaviors about the institution? A place to begin is to recast the mental models that have been created over time. Mental models, as defined by Senge (1990), are deeply held internal images of how the world works. For many, these models may be simple generalizations, attitudes, or beliefs that shape how we interpret the world. For many of us, our mental models exist but we are entirely unaware how they color our view of reality. They are present just below our consciousness.

The belief that a college or university is a commuter institution can become a deeply embedded mental model. Everyone within the system uses the commuter model as the lens to filter the events and activities that define the institution. It is no wonder that with such a powerful model guiding our vision, administrators, faculty, and students behave in a manner to perpetuate the prevailing representation of the college or university. It deters new insights and learning from forming about how to transform the campus into an exciting and involving environment for all members.

This is a key challenge for the student affairs researcher—to use assessment and research to alter the prevailing mental models. Only when those mental models are dismantled can new ones emerge. When they do, new systems can follow to promote learning and redefine the nature of campus.

This is far easier to describe than it is to implement. Nevertheless, let us return to the predominate mental model discussed earlier, the commuter institution. What kinds of assessment information can refute the commuter-oriented mind set? One approach is to conduct a qualitative examination of students who may be labeled as commuters. Such an in-depth examination, not bound by preconceived biases or the tendency to reduce a student's experiences into discrete numerical responses on a survey form, may help cast a new light on students' experiences on or off campus.

We may discover that students spend considerable time on or near campus. In fact, we may find that students whom we label as commuters may in fact be students living in the neighborhoods adjoining the campus who rarely take advantage of campus resources because they, too, perceive the institution to be commuter oriented!

We also may learn that the same students invest considerable time in activities that are more important to them—their jobs, volunteer work in the community, family or relationships off campus. Commuter students are not disinterested in the institution, nor are they apathetic; they expend their energies in the activities that they value and that provide them with the most satisfaction. Their lack of involvement in campus life should not be interpreted as a character flaw or a personal inadequacy. Their lives are challenging and full without being involved on campus.

This is only one example in which the student affairs researcher can reframe mental models. Many other assessment approaches should be added that challenge prevailing assumptions. Student affairs researchers need to be creative and broaden their repertoire of assessment methods to effectively dismantle mental models that inhibit new organizational learning. The information broker should be able to weave multiple sources of assessment findings and data into a richly textured quilt that encourages new insights and leads to deeper, richer understanding.

Implications for Student Affairs Researchers

Senge's five components of a learning organization provide a new approach to reconceptualize student affairs research. On a practical level, there are many implications for how student affairs researchers conduct their work to help create a learning organization.

Using Data to Encourage Discussions, Not to Analyze Problems. To alter existing mental models, the student affairs researcher must use data strategically to help create conditions for broad, participatory discussions. As Senge proposed, groups learn and generate new insights and understandings far better than individuals working alone. This means reframing how to share results of assessment or evaluation activities. Findings cannot be prescriptive or designed to place blame. The best kind of assessment captures the attention of the intended audience, offers thought-provoking insights, and generates new questions that act to start discussion and ultimately enhance organizational learning. The student affairs researcher truly becomes a broker of assessment information.

Sharing Information Builds Trust and Credibility. One can only engage others in purposeful learning if the assessment information is packaged and prepared in a manner that will be easily accepted by its intended readers or audience. At the same time, the researcher must be willing to share the whole story, the good news and the bad.

When information is not readily shared or there is a perception that findings are only presenting a partial picture, the assessment effort and the messenger lose integrity. Without trust, others within the organization will not risk dismantling their mental models. To encourage dialogue that leads to new insights, the assessment process must be open and participatory. All members of the organization should have access to the information, and it should be formatted in a way that is easily understood.

Anticipating Cultural Shifts in the Institution. Student affairs researchers cannot be reactive in the institutional setting. Often the best assessment activities have the most impact when they are done as a "triggering mechanism." An important job of the student affairs researcher is to anticipate when members of the institution are prepared and ready for a new assessment initiative, or to have information ready in response to when there is a new interest in a particular set of issues or concerns. Timing for the student affairs researcher is critical.

During the interval between establishing a consensus to engage in a research project and completing the work, enthusiasm and interest can wane. The effective student affairs researcher should anticipate the prevailing interests of the campus and have information ready while the organizational culture is most curious.

Brokering Means Transmitting Credible Information, Not Generating It. We live in an era in which the real challenges are not in the creation of new information but in finding ways to assimilate information and make it meaningful. Student affairs researchers should take advantage of all the credible sources of information within and outside the institution, including their own, as they look for patterns and extend new insights.

With the explosion of the Internet and new computer software, the ability to carry out assessment and disseminate findings has become far easier. The drudgery of data management and analysis has also been reduced. This may increase the amount the information available, but it does not ensure meaningfulness. As an information broker, the student affairs researcher must have the acuity to know when their data or assessment sources are principled, valid, and reliable.

Concluding Thoughts

Pat Cross, in an address to the American College Personnel Association, offered a direct challenge to student affairs professionals when she said, "My prescription for new lenses for today's campus professionals, and in particular for student affairs professionals, then calls for a clear focus on student learning in all of its dimensions. Learning is, after all, the goal of all education, and it is through a lens that focuses on learning that we must ultimately examine and judge our effectiveness as educators" (Cross, 1996, p. 9). Senge would probably agree.

The same challenge exists for those engaged in student affairs research. How can we use our research tools, unique position within the organization, and capacity to "see the trees and forests" to create the conditions in which organizational learning can really take place? Only under these conditions can the student affairs researcher become an information broker and an agent for organizational learning within the student affairs and the institution.

References

American College Personnel Association, *The Student Affairs Learning Imperative: Implications for Student Affairs.* Washington, D.C.: American College Personnel Association, 1996.

Cross, K. P. "New Lenses on Learning," *About Campus,* 1996, *1*(1), 4–9.

Miller, T. K. (ed.). "Outcomes Assessment and Program Evaluation." In *Council for the Advancement of Standards in Higher Education: The Book of Professional Standards for Higher Education.* Washington, D.C.: Council for the Advancement of Standards in Higher Education, 1997.

Senge, P. M. *The Fifth Discipline: The Art and Practice of the Learning Organization.* New York: Doubleday, 1990.

THOMAS D. HADLEY is associate vice president of student affairs at the University of Cincinnati.

Print- and World-Wide-Web-based resources for student affairs researchers are discussed.

Resources for Student Affairs Researchers

Gary D. Malaney

There is no "how to" book for student affairs researchers. Although this volume provides some insights into the research practices of some student affairs research offices, it will not make anyone a student affairs researcher. In reality, a student affairs researcher is a social scientist, and the practice of good social science research is not something one can learn overnight or by reading a couple of books. In my opinion, the only way to become a good social science researcher is to enroll in an advanced degree program in social science research and then engage in the practice of research under the watchful eye of a mentor, preferably in a research office.

A good social science researcher needs to understand several research methodologies, both quantitative and qualitative, such as survey design and focus group research, and the researcher needs to know how to select the right design to answer a specific research question. Also, in student affairs, a researcher needs to have a basic understanding of program evaluation and assessment. It takes years of research study and practice to become proficient in conducting research, analyzing data, and communicating the findings. Given the limited space of this chapter, I could not begin to offer everything one would need to know. My intent here is to offer some direction on where to find valuable resources that will enable newcomers to begin their journeys and veterans to possibly discover new avenues.

Resources in Print

There are many texts on social science research methods, and undoubtedly reading a couple of these books is essential. All of the social science research texts cover basically the same ground, so I do not think the actual choice of texts is that important. The text *Research Methods in the Social Sciences* by Chava Frankfort-Nachmias and David Nachmias (1996) is very thorough.

In addition to general texts on research methods, student affairs researchers need to have a solid knowledge of survey research methodology. Several excellent texts are available, such as Rossi, Wright, and Anderson's (1985) *Handbook of Survey Research.* Also, for mail and telephone surveys, Dilman's (1978) work is a classic. In addition, Sage publishes a very hands-on, applied "Survey Kit" consisting of nine paperback books that discuss questionnaire design, sampling, data analysis, and report writing.

The Survey Kit follows the same kind of structure as Sage's Program Evaluation Kit, another collection of small paperback books designed to assist individuals in the art and science of program evaluation. I think this kit is a must for individuals just beginning to get involved in program evaluation.

The one problem with most of the books mentioned above is that they are short on examples from the field of higher education. A simpler book that is geared toward higher education is offered by Light, Singer, and Willet (1990). Most of the examples in this book pertain to studying undergraduate student populations.

In Chapter One, I mentioned some key works pertaining to student affairs research. These books include Kuh's (1979) work on evaluation, as well as books by Beeler and Hunter (1991) and Upcraft and Schuh (1996). In addition to reading these books, researchers need to read the journals associated with student affairs, such as the *NASPA Journal* and the *Journal of College Student Development,* both of which discuss research related to student affairs (for example, see Malaney, 1993; Moxley, 1988). There also are numerous journals related to specific interests in student affairs, such as residence life and student activities. Though these journals typically are less research oriented, an occasional article of significance may be found. Student affairs researchers must also read the important research journals in the field of higher education: *Research in Higher Education, The Review of Higher Education,* and *The Journal of Higher Education.* These journals often include research studies related to students.

One other research area of growing interest is student outcomes assessment. Although Upcraft and Schuh (1996) discussed this area in some detail, their book is more focused on assessing student life outside of the classroom. Given the current interest in assessment of academic learning, student affairs researchers also need to have an understanding of academic assessment, especially to make sure that student learning outside the classroom is included in campus assessment agendas that might be focused only on classroom learning. Dary Erwin (1991) wrote an important book that looks at this combined context. Astin (1993) and Banta (1993) also have authored excellent books that discuss outcomes assessment.

Web-Based Resources

Probably most readers of this book are familiar with the vast resources available on the World Wide Web. One of the growing problems with the Web is that there are so many resources, many individuals do not know where to begin to look for assistance. For student affairs researchers, there are a few valuable resources that I discuss briefly here. Some of these websites also were mentioned in Chapter Six of this volume.

First, the ERIC (Educational Resources Information Center) Clearinghouse on Higher Education Website (www.gwu.edu/~eriche) offers vast information pertaining to higher education, including a library offering full-text documents on specific issues. The site also provides on-line access to the ERIC database that allows a researcher to locate abstracts from educational journals, books, reports from individual colleges, and conference papers. Many of the non-journal materials can be ordered on-line. The website also provides listings of colleges and universities and higher education professional organizations, such as the Association for Institutional Research (www.fsu.edu/~air/home.htm), another valuable resource for student affairs researchers. The ERIC website also has a subsite directly related to assessment and evaluation (ericae.net/). A researcher could easily spend several hours investigating the materials available on the entire ERIC website.

Another important website for student affairs researchers is the Student Affairs Virtual Compass (www.StudentAffairs.com/). This site provides listings for and links to areas such as student affairs professional organizations, job listings in student affairs, and on-line journals. The Virtual Compass provides a listing for listservs in various student affairs areas and instructions on how to join such listservs. There also is a list of functional areas in student affairs where information and links are provided. One such link is to the Student Affairs Research site (www.uncc.edu/stuaffairs/sarlinks.htm), where links are provided to existing campus-based student affairs research sites, including my own (www-saris.admin.umass.edu/saris/). Some of these sites provide comprehensive information on what individual campuses are doing in student affairs research.

References

Astin, A. W. *Assessment for Excellence: The Philosophy and Practice of Assessment and Evaluation in Higher Education.* Phoenix: Oryx Press, 1993.

Banta, T. W. *Making a Difference: Outcomes of a Decade of Assessment in Higher Education.* San Francisco: Jossey-Bass, 1993.

Beeler, K. J., and Hunter, D. E. *Puzzles and Pieces in Wonderland: The Promise and Practice of Student Affairs Research.* Washington, D.C.: NASPA, 1991.

Dilman, D. A. *Mail and Telephone Surveys: The Total Design Method.* New York: Wiley, 1978.

Erwin, T. D. *Assessing Student Learning and Development: A Guide to the Principles, Goals, and Methods of Determining College Outcomes.* San Francisco: Jossey-Bass, 1991.

Frankfort-Nachmias, C., and Nachmias, D. *Research Methods in the Social Sciences.* 5th ed. New York: St. Martins, 1996.

Kuh, G. D. *Evaluation in Student Affairs.* Cincinnati, Ohio: ACPA Media, 1979.

Light, R. J., Singer, J. D., and Willet, J. B. *By Design: Planning Research on Higher Education.* Cambridge, Mass.: Harvard University Press, 1990.

Malaney, G. D. "A Comprehensive Student Affairs Research Office." *NASPA Journal,* 1993, *30,* 182–189.

Moxley, L. S. "The Role and Impact of a Student Affairs Research and Evaluation Office." *NASPA Journal,* 1988, *25,* 174–179.

Rossi, P. H., Wright, J. W., and Anderson, A. (eds.) *Handbook of Survey Research.* Orlando: Academic Press, 1985.

Upcraft, M. L., and Schuh, J. H. *Assessment in Student Affairs: A Guide for Practitioners.* San Francisco: Jossey-Bass, 1996.

GARY D. MALANEY is director of Student Affairs Research, Information, and Systems (SARIS) and associate professor of higher education at the University of Massachusetts Amherst.

INDEX

Back Issue/Subscription Order Form

Copy or detach and send to:
Jossey-Bass Inc., Publishers, 350 Sansome Street, San Francisco CA 94104-1342

Call or fax toll free!
Phone 888-378-2537 6AM-5PM PST; Fax 800-605-2665

Back issues: Please send me the following issues at $23 each.
(Important: please include series initials and issue number, such as SS90.)

1. SS _____

_____

_____

$ _____ Total for single issues

$ _____ Shipping charges (for single issues *only;* subscriptions are exempt from shipping charges): Up to $30, add $5^{50} • $30^{01}–$50, add $6^{50} $50^{01}–$75, add $7^{50} • $75^{01}–$100, add $9 • $100^{01}–$150, add $10 Over $150, call for shipping charge.

Subscriptions Please ❏ start ❏ renew my subscription to *New Directions for Student Services* for the year 19___ at the following rate:

❏ Individual $56 ❏ Institutional $99

NOTE: Subscriptions are quarterly, and are for the calendar year only. Subscriptions begin with the spring issue of the year indicated above. For shipping outside the U.S., please add $25.

$ _____ Total single issues and subscriptions (CA, IN, NJ, NY, and DC residents, add sales tax for single issues. NY and DC residents must include shipping charges when calculating sales tax. NY and Canadian residents only, add sales tax for subscriptions.)

❏ Payment enclosed (U.S. check or money order only)
❏ VISA, MC, AmEx, Discover Card #_____ Exp. date_____

Signature _____ Day phone _____
❏ Bill me (U.S. institutional orders only. Purchase order required.)
Purchase order #_____

Name _____

Address _____

_____

_____

Phone_____ E-mail _____

For more information about Jossey-Bass Publishers, visit our Web site at:
www.josseybass.com **PRIORITY CODE = ND1**

OTHER TITLES AVAILABLE IN THE
NEW DIRECTIONS FOR STUDENT SERVICES SERIES
John H. Schuh, Editor-in-Chief
Elizabeth J. Whitt, Associate Editor

UNITED STATES POSTAL SERVICE™

Statement of Ownership, Management, and Circulation
(Required by 39 USC 3685)

1. Publication Title	2. Publication Number	3. Filing Date
NEW DIRECTIONS FOR STUDENT SERVICES	0 1 6 4 . 7 9 7 0	10/14/98

4. Issue Frequency	5. Number of Issues Published Annually	6. Annual Subscription Price
QUARTERLY	4	$56 – indiv. $99 – instit.

7. Complete Mailing Address of Known Office of Publication *(Not printer)* *(Street, city, county, state, and ZIP+4)*
350 SANSOME STREET
SAN FRANCISCO, CA   94104
(SAN FRANCISCO COUNTY)

Contact Person
ROGER HUNT
Telephone
415 782 3232

8. Complete Mailing Address of Headquarters or General Business Office of Publisher *(Not printer)*

SAME AS ABOVE

9. Full Names and Complete Mailing Addresses of Publisher, Editor, and Managing Editor *(Do not leave blank)*

Publisher *(Name and complete mailing address)*
JOSSEY-BASS INC., PUBLISHERS
(ABOVE ADDRESS)

Editor *(Name and complete mailing address)* JOHN SCHUH, PROFESSOR
PROFESSIONAL STUDIES IN EDUCATION
IOWA STATE UNIV/LAGOMARCINO HALL N247E
AMES, IA   50011

Managing Editor *(Name and complete mailing address)*

NONE

10. Owner *(Do not leave blank. If the publication is owned by a corporation, give the name and address of the corporation immediately followed by the names and addresses of all stockholders owning or holding 1 percent or more of the total amount of stock. If not owned by a corporation, give the names and addresses of the individual owners. If owned by a partnership or other unincorporated firm, give its name and address as well as those of each individual owner. If the publication is published by a nonprofit organization, give its name and address.)*

Full Name	Complete Mailing Address
SIMON & SCHUSTER	P.O. BOX 1172
	ENGLEWOOD CLIFFS, NJ 07632-1172

11. Known Bondholders, Mortgagees, and Other Security Holders Owning or Holding 1 Percent or More of Total Amount of Bonds, Mortgages, or Other Securities. If none, check box ▶ ☐ None

Full Name	Complete Mailing Address
SAME AS ABOVE	SAME AS ABOVE

12. Tax Status *(For completion by nonprofit organizations authorized to mail at special rates)* *(Check one)*
The purpose, function, and nonprofit status of this organization and the exempt status for federal income tax purposes:
☐ Has Not Changed During Preceding 12 Months
☐ Has Changed During Preceding 12 Months *(Publisher must submit explanation of change with this statement)*

PS Form **3526**, September 1995   *(See Instructions on Reverse)*

---

13. Publication Title	14. Issue Date for Circulation Data Below
NEW DIRECTIONS FOR STUDENT SERVICES	FALL 1998

15.	Extent and Nature of Circulation	Average No. Copies Each Issue During Preceding 12 Months	Actual No. Copies of Single Issue Published Nearest to Filing Date
a. Total Number of Copies *(Net press run)*		1892	1902
b. Paid and/or Requested Circulation	(1) Sales Through Dealers and Carriers, Street Vendors, and Counter Sales *(Not mailed)*	207	47
	(2) Paid or Requested Mail Subscriptions *(Include advertiser's proof copies and exchange copies)*	786	846
c. Total Paid and/or Requested Circulation *(Sum of 15b(1) and 15b(2))* ▶		993	893
d. Free Distribution by Mail *(Samples, complimentary, and other free)*		0	0
e. Free Distribution Outside the Mail *(Carriers or other means)*		140	76
f. Total Free Distribution *(Sum of 15d and 15e)* ▶		140	76
g. Total Distribution *(Sum of 15c and 15f)* ▶		1133	969
h. Copies not Distributed	(1) Office Use, Leftovers, Spoiled	759	933
	(2) Returns from News Agents	0	0
i. Total *(Sum of 15g, 15h(1), and 15h(2))* ▶		1892	1902
Percent Paid and/or Requested Circulation *(15c / 15g x 100)*		88%	92%

16. Publication of Statement of Ownership
☒ Publication required. Will be printed in the WINTER 1998 issue of this publication.
☐ Publication not required.

17. Signature and Title of Editor, Publisher, Business Manager, or Owner

[signature] SUSAN E. LEWIS
DIRECTOR OF PERIODICALS

Date
10/14/98

I certify that all information furnished on this form is true and complete. I understand that anyone who furnishes false or misleading information on this form or who omits material or information requested on the form may be subject to criminal sanctions (including fines and imprisonment) and/or civil sanctions (including multiple damages and civil penalties).

Instructions to Publishers

1. Complete and file one copy of this form with your postmaster annually on or before October 1. Keep a copy of the completed form for your records.

2. In cases where the stockholder or security holder is a trustee, include in items 10 and 11 the name of the person or corporation for whom the trustee is acting. Also include the names and addresses of individuals who are stockholders who own or hold 1 percent or more of the total amount of bonds, mortgages, or other securities of the publishing corporation. In item 11, if none, check the box. Use blank sheets if more space is required.

3. Be sure to furnish all circulation information called for in item 15. Free circulation must be shown in items 15d, e, and f.

4. If the publication had second-class authorization as a general or requester publication, this Statement of Ownership, Management, and Circulation must be published; it must be printed in any issue in October or, if the publication is not published during October, the first issue printed after October.

5. In item 16, indicate the date of the issue in which this Statement of Ownership will be published.

6. Item 17 must be signed.

Failure to file or publish a statement of ownership may lead to suspension of second-class authorization.

PS Form **3526**, September 1995 *(Reverse)*